CITYSPOTS
SINGA

WHAT'S IN YOUR GUIDEBOOK

WHAT'S IN YOUR GUIDEBOOK?

Independent authors Impartial up-to-date information from our travel experts who meticulously source local knowledge.

Experience Thomas Cook's 165 years in the travel industry and guidebook publishing enriches every word with expertise you can trust.

Travel know-how Thomas Cook has thousands of staff working around the globe, all living and breathing travel.

Editors Travel-publishing professionals, pulling everything together to craft a perfect blend of words, pictures, maps and design.

You, the traveller We deliver a practical, no-nonsense approach to information, geared to how you really use it.

CITYSPOTS
SINGAPORE

Written by Pat Levy
Updated by Jill Thomas

Published by Thomas Cook Publishing
A division of Thomas Cook Tour Operations Limited
Company registration No: 3772199 England
The Thomas Cook Business Park, 9 Coningsby Road
Peterborough PE3 8SB, United Kingdom
Email: books@thomascook.com, Tel: +44 (0)1733 416477
www.thomascookpublishing.com

Produced by The Content Works Ltd
Aston Court, Kingsmead Business Park, Frederick Place
High Wycombe, Bucks HP11 1LA
www.thecontentworks.com

Series design based on an original concept by Studio 183 Limited

ISBN: 978-1-84848-176-3

First edition © 2007 Thomas Cook Publishing
This second edition © 2009 Thomas Cook Publishing
Text © Thomas Cook Publishing
Maps © Thomas Cook Publishing/PCGraphics (UK) Limited
Transport map © Communicarta Limited

Series Editor: Lucy Armstrong
Production/DTP: Steven Collins

Printed and bound in Spain by GraphyCems

Cover photography (The roofs of Thian Hock Keng Temple and the business district)
© SIME/kaos02/4Corners Images

All rights reserved. No part of this publication may be reproduced, stored in a retrieval system or transmitted, in any form or any means, electronic, mechanical, recording or otherwise, in any part of the world, without prior permission of the publisher. Requests for permission should be made to the publisher at the above address.

Although every care has been taken in compiling this publication, and the contents are believed to be correct at the time of printing, Thomas Cook Tour Operations Limited cannot accept any responsibility for errors or omission, however caused, or for changes in details given in the guidebook, or for the consequences of any reliance on the information provided. Descriptions and assessments are based on the author's views and experiences when writing and do not necessarily represent those of Thomas Cook Tour Operations Limited.

CONTENTS

INTRODUCING SINGAPORE

Introduction..............................8
When to go 10
Thaipusam..............................14
History....................................16
Lifestyle..................................18
Culture....................................20

MAKING THE MOST OF SINGAPORE

Shopping................................24
Eating & drinking..................26
Entertainment
 & nightlife 30
Sport & relaxation 34
Accommodation 37
The best of Singapore 42
Suggested itineraries 44
Something for nothing 46
When it rains 48
On arrival...............................50

THE CITY OF SINGAPORE

Orchard Road &
 Colonial District 60
Little India & Arab Street 76
Boat Quay & Chinatown 90

OUT OF TOWN TRIPS

Sentosa & Western
 Singapore..........................104
Bukit Timah,
 Changi & Bintan................116

PRACTICAL INFORMATION

Directory 126
Emergencies 138

INDEX 140

MAPS

Singapore...............................52
Singapore transport map....56
Orchard Road &
 Colonial District.................62
Little India & Arab Street 78
Boat Quay & Chinatown......92
Singapore region.................106

CITYSPOTS

SYMBOLS KEY

The following symbols are used throughout this book:

a address t telephone w website address L opening times
public transport connections important

The following symbols are used on the maps:
- information office
- airport
- hospital
- police station
- bus station
- railway station
- MRT stop
- cathedral
- points of interest
- O city
- O large town
- ○ small town
- motorway
- main road
- minor road
- railway
- numbers denote featured cafés & restaurants

Hotels and restaurants are graded by approximate price as follows:
£ budget price ££ mid-range price £££ expensive

Singapore's skyline

INTRODUCING Singapore

INTRODUCING SINGAPORE

Introduction

There's a kind of unreal quality to your first few minutes in Singapore. You will probably arrive at the end of a long-haul flight feeling a little jaded, and it is blissful to glide calmly through the air-conditioned atmosphere of the arrivals lounge. But beware: its vast size and the bustle of people can have a soporific effect, making you unready for the moment you exit into the real atmosphere of the place and have the sudden feeling of being slapped in the face by a hot wet face flannel.

However, that will be your biggest shock because Singapore works – the cliché is that it works too well – and this helps make it the perfect short-stay destination. On shiny new public transport (don't put your feet up on the seats, eat or drink or, heavens forefend, drop your bubble gum on the floor) or in a swanky limousine you will cruise through the manicured expressways – no one exceeding the speed limit – to the perfect city, a wonderful amalgam of the so new they haven't taken the wrapping off yet and the beautifully preserved and renovated buildings and streets of old.

Everything you ever wanted is here – great hotels, courteous staff, bedazzling food options, shops and exotic markets, nightclubs, history, and a brief ride away raw nature with fabulous animals and plants, tiny unspoiled islands, sandy beaches and an entire island dedicated to fun.

If it's sun you want, there's more than enough and most afternoons a blessed shower hits the place to cool it all down. If you don't like the heat, with a bit of planning you need never step outside yet still have fun. If all that sounds a bit Stepford,

INTRODUCTION

rest assured that, while you might go crazy if you had to live here for long, a holiday here is just perfect.

◆ *The glitz of Singapore at night*

INTRODUCING SINGAPORE

When to go

SEASONS & CLIMATE

Only 136 km (85 miles) north of the equator, Singapore has no seasons; it is hot and humid all year round. Temperatures rarely fall below 21°C (70°F) and peak at around 32°C (90°F) or a little more. Humidity is around 90 per cent. Rain is a regular part of most days, falling in a burst often accompanied by thunderstorms and lasting between 30 minutes and two hours. December and January tend to be a little wetter than other months.

● *Singapore's Dragon Boat Festival is a great spectacle*

WHEN TO GO

ANNUAL EVENTS
January–February
New Year Suntec City and Sentosa are the places to be, with firework displays, street performers and more.

Chinese New Year For several weeks leading up to the event there are decorations and lights around the city. Children are given red envelopes containing money, and families go visiting. On the river there is a celebration of the signs of the Chinese zodiac, featuring whichever animal is in ascendance in that particular year. On New Year's Day the Chingay Parade travels from City Hall to Suntec City and features street performers, acrobats, dragon dance troupes, beauty queens and gymnastic displays from all over the world. On New Year's Day the shops and sights are likely to be closed.

Thaipusam (see pages 14–15).

March–April
Qing Ming Festival Families visit temples to light offerings and bring food to their ancestors. The best place to observe the ceremonies is Kong Meng San Phor Kark See Temple at Sin Ming Road.

May–June
Dragon Boat Festival Rice dumplings are sold all over town and rowers compete in the dragon boat races across Marina Bay.

Vesak Day Celebration of the birth of the Buddha. Temples release caged birds and there are candlelit processions in the evening.

August–September

Festival of the Hungry Ghosts For a month bad spirits are released from hell and walk the earth. To appease them, incense, fake banknotes and paper replicas of consumer goods are burned and offerings of food are made in little makeshift shrines all over the city. There are lots of Chinese street operas throughout the month.

National Day Grand multicultural parade followed by speeches and fireworks at the National Stadium.

Ramadan The Muslim month of fasting. In the evenings at sundown when the fast is broken there are stalls around the mosques selling delicacies. Best visited at The Sultan Mosque in Arab Street or in Geylang. The last day of Ramadan, Hari Raya Puasa, is celebrated with new clothes and visits to family.

Womad Four days of concerts and performances in Fort Canning Park.

Singapore Grand Prix A buzzing three-day event in September in the Marina Bay area that's distinguished by being the world's first-ever night race. Ⓦ www.singaporegp.sg

Moon Cake Festival Moon cakes are sold all over the city and children carry paper lanterns. Best seen in the Chinese Gardens in Jurong, where enormous lanterns are on display and dragon dances and other performances take place.

October–November

Deepavali The Hindu Festival of Lights. Serangoon Road is filled with street markets and bazaars, prayers in the temples, and lots and lots of lights.

Festival of the Nine Emperor Gods Procession in Serangoon

Road from the Kiu Ong Yiah Temple. Opera performances and spirit mediums accompany the effigies of the gods.
Navarathiri This month-long Hindu festival sees performances of classical dance and music in Hindu temples all over the city, but especially at the Sri Thandayuthapani Temple on Tank Road. On the final evening a procession led by a silver horse travels around the city.
Thimithi Hindu devotees run barefoot across hot coals at the Sri Mariamman Temple in Chinatown.

December
Christmas Day Tinsel, Chinese Santas, Rudolph, lights and parcels. No change there then.
Hari Raya Haji The celebration of the return of devotees from Mecca.

PUBLIC HOLIDAYS
New Year's Day 1 Jan
Chinese New Year late Jan/early Feb
Good Friday 2 Apr 2010, 22 Apr 2011, 6 Apr 2012
Labour Day 1 May
Vesak Day May
National Day 9 Aug
Hari Raya Puasa Aug/Sept
Deepavali Oct/Nov
Hari Raya Haji Dec
Christmas Day 25 Dec

INTRODUCING SINGAPORE

Thaipusam

Thaipusam takes place in late January/early February in the Hindu month of Thai when the constellation of Pusam is in the ascendant. The festival is practised all over Malaysia but has been banned in India.

The celebration honours the story of Iduban, a devotee of the Lord Murugan who decided to show his love for the god by climbing a mountain carrying offerings of milk and honey. Murugan chose to put obstacles in his path. Despite this, Iduban reached the top and was given a place in heaven at the god's side.

Devotees – often those who wish to ask the god for something (good health, passing an exam, children) – imitate Iduban's journey by walking from the Sri Srinivasa Perumal Temple (see page 81) in Serangoon Road to the Chettiar Temple in Tank Road. The stunning, not to say shocking, manner in which they do this makes this the strangest yet most compelling festival in the city.

Devotees (mostly men) do this ritual at least twice, preparing themselves for weeks in advance with a special diet, abstinence from comforts and special prayers. Entering into a trance-like state, they pierce their mouths with skewers, hang pots of milk and honey by hooks from their flesh and carry huge steel frames called *kavadis* on their shoulders, held in place by more skewers and hooks.

The whole family turns out to help the devotee on their way and shower them with turmeric-coloured water, milk and honey. The long walk in Singapore's oppressive heat lasts for several hours.

Devotees are happy to be photographed (or perhaps they don't notice). Also, you can go into the Sri Srinivasa Perumal

THAIPUSAM

Temple to watch the preparations or stand along the route and admire the dedication of the devotees and their families.

▲ *A devotee at Thaipusam*

INTRODUCING SINGAPORE

History

Singapore's history begins around the 14th century with records of the island, named Temasek, as a small trading post on a swampy, malaria- and tiger-infested isle.

Fought over by Javanese and Thai empires, the island languished then until 1819 when the Briton Thomas Stamford Raffles, impressed by the possibilities its deep water bay and wide river mouth offered, decided that this would be a good place for a trading post. Negotiations with the sultan of Melaka were followed by a massive immigration of workers, chiefly from China, for the emerging docks.

By 1824 the island was bought outright and in 1867 it became part of the British Crown Colony called the Straits Settlements. Grand buildings arose, areas of land were earmarked for each of the ethnic communities and by the end of the 19th century Singapore dominated trade in the region.

All was going well until World War II changed things forever. Singapore became a strategic military outpost, holding the line against the encroaching Japanese armies cycling down through the Malay peninsula. The British surrendered the island in 1942. There followed some legendary cruelties on behalf of the occupying forces, murdering as many as 25,000 Chinese men and interning and causing the deaths from disease and malnutrition of hundreds of Allied soldiers and European civilians.

In 1945 the British sheepishly took back what was theirs, but things were never the same. During the 1950s various groups in Malaya began a struggle for independence from

HISTORY

Britain, which they achieved in 1957. Singapore was still British but now had an elected legislature and, in 1959, after Lee Kuan Yew's People's Action Party took the majority of seats, it joined the Malay Federation.

By 1965 Singapore was asked to leave by the other states after racial and political tensions led to riots between Chinese and Malays. Singapore suddenly found itself an independent state and despite all the odds – no natural resources, few industries – went from strength to economic strength, developing its port facilities, financial services, IT industry and refineries; building swathes of roads, public housing and hospitals; and creating a compulsory system of social welfare contributions (the Central Provident Fund) for every citizen. It also had massive artistic and political censorship, population control policies that worked too well (threatening the Chinese with becoming fewer in relation to other ethnic groups) and no opposition parties to speak of.

Modern Singapore has lightened up a little – although locals laugh ruefully at some of the legislation they live with every day. There are enforced fines for littering, jaywalking, urinating in lifts and eating on the MRT (Mass Rapid Transit) and there are still large numbers of people executed by the state each year. Visitors are often confused about the legality of chewing gum. The chewing of gum is allowed if you can prove it's for therapeutic purposes (for example, to quit smoking). The import and sale of chewing gum (except for such 'therapeutic gum') is illegal and subject to a fine; as is throwing it anywhere other than in a bin.

INTRODUCING SINGAPORE

Lifestyle

What a strange country Singapore is. From the moment you step out of the airport everything is manicured and well behaved, and everything, it seems at times, has a price. Those Singaporeans who buy into the system laughingly admit to the mantra of the 5Cs: cash, condo, career, car, credit card. A sixth 'C' – children – comes a long way down the line.

The young, upwardly mobile Singaporean is well educated, has a shopping list of requirements and a timetable. Many have little or no time for a social life and, particularly Chinese 20-somethings, attend government sponsored get-togethers where they can meet partners with a similar shopping list to their own. Around 13 per cent of Singaporeans are millionaires and fewer than half of the population were born on the island.

Once in charge of their condo, credit card and car, Singaporeans have time to start enjoying life a little more. Many employ a maid from Indonesia or the Philippines. Eating out is not part of their mantra, it being more like an essential such as breathing or shopping. Most Singaporeans greet their friends with the expression 'Have you eaten?' rather than 'Hello'.

Everyone in Singapore, regardless of income, has strong opinions on places to eat out – where the best hawker centres (see page 28) are, where the best *laksa* can be found, who makes the flakiest *roti*, which pizza place allows you to stack up your salad bowl highest and which all-you-can-eat buffets don't weigh the food you leave on your plate and charge you for it.

Singaporeans love to eat seafood and will travel a long way and in difficult circumstances to get it. At weekends tiny wooden

LIFESTYLE

shacks along the Johor coast and on the offshore islands fill up with busloads of people after their special dish, be it drunken prawns or chilli crab.

Shopping, the second most practised activity on the island, is also a major topic for discussion over the dinner table. Each mall has its area of excellence and new malls are visited by families much as a new tourist destination.

Whatever activities they engage in, Singaporeans are both proud of and able to laugh at their country and its peculiar ways.

The popular Maxwell Food Centre

INTRODUCING SINGAPORE

Culture

With three ethnic groups, Singapore has an amazing wealth of culture to call on. Around 75 per cent of the population is Chinese, 14 per cent Malay and 9 per cent Indian. The old ways of each culture are dwindling a little as each generation becomes more Singaporean, but certain features remain.

Chinese opera can be found at fairly impromptu locations at most times of the year but especially during the month of the Hungry Ghosts (see page 12), and stages appear overnight in suburban centres and marketplaces. The opera is a strange combination of slapstick, singing music and melodrama, enacted in Cantonese or Hokkien, the dressing room being the back of a lorry and the stage a rickety set of planks. The make-up and costume, accompanying music and singing are unmissable.

In shopping centres, usually around Chinese New Year (see page 11), you'll find the city's lion dancers. Generally formed from martial arts groups, the team of lion dancers (usually two men to a lion) and their accompanying musicians perform acrobatic dances, with firecrackers and cymbal crashing to drive out the spirits of the old year.

Indian classical music and dance are strong in the city and can be seen performed in many of its temples during religious festivals. Malay culture is more homely and less public, but there are performances of Malay dance and music at Istana Kampong Glam (page 80).

For more contemporary culture, the Theatres on the Bay are the best place to look. Concerts of classical and modern music as well as drama, both local and imported, are shown there.

CULTURE

🔺 *The Victoria Theatre hosts regular concerts*

INTRODUCING SINGAPORE

During the summer there are performances of all kinds at Fort Canning Hill and other parks (w www.nparks.gov.sg).

The Victoria Theatre (@ 9 Empress Palace ❶ 6338 8283), the **Arts House** (@ 1 Old Parliament Lane ❶ 6332 6900) and **Suntec City** (@ 1 Raffles Blvd ❶ 6337 2888) are venues for cultural performances. Other arts venues include the **Drama Centre at the National Library** (@ 3F National Library, 100 Victoria St ❶ 6837 8400), **Substation** (@ 45 Armenian St ❶ 6337 7800) and the **DBS Drama Centre** (@ 20 Merbau Rd ❶ 6837 8400).

The **Singapore Symphony Orchestra** (w www.sso.org.sg) offers regular performances of the classics and popular music, while the **Singapore Chinese Orchestra** (w www.sco.com.sg) and performance groups from the Nanyang Academy of Fine Arts also have regular offerings. Occasionally the **Singapore Indoor Stadium** (@ 2 Stadium Walk ❶ 6344 2660) plays host to major productions from abroad.

The **Singapore Art Museum** (@ 71 Bras Basah Rd ❶ 6332 3222), the Science Centre (see page 111) and the Esplanade Tunnel (from Empress Place to Esplanade Park and Esplanade Theatres) regularly feature art exhibitions, and there are tens of small private art galleries throughout the city such as **Sculpture Square** (@ 155 Middle Rd ❶ 6333 1055), **Singapore Tyler Print Institute** (@ 41 Robertson Quay ❶ 6336 3663) and the **Opera Gallery** (@ 391 Orchard Rd ❶ 6735 2618). Public art includes several pieces by Roy Lichtenstein (called Singapore Brushstrokes) along the Millennia Walk. May sees the annual Singapore Arts Festival (w www.singaporeartsfest.com).

▶ *Singapore harbour and city at night*

MAKING THE MOST OF
Singapore

MAKING THE MOST OF SINGAPORE

Shopping

If shopping was an Olympic sport, Singapore would win the gold, silver and bronze every time. Shopping is a major pastime and entire families will cheerfully troop out to Orchard Road or one of the other shopping centres to make a whole day of it. They'll eat in one of the food halls, take in a movie and only come home when all possibilities have been exhausted.

For visitors the problem will be how to make room in your luggage for the beautiful things you can buy at relatively low prices.

Fashionistas should check out Singapore's designers as well as the usual suspects. Good places to look for local designers are Bugis Junction, Far East Plaza and An Siang Hill in Chinatown. Names to look out for are Francis Cheong, Madeleine Wong and her Posse label, and K Mi Huang.

Tailor-made suits are an interesting option, although if you're travelling on to Bangkok or Hong Kong you'll get better deals in those places. Sarongs and saris, silk, batik and other fabrics can be found in Arab Street or Serangoon Road.

Jewellery is abundant and outside of the big department stores its price is negotiable. Look out for good gold items and semi-precious stones, particularly jade.

Singapore excels in arts and crafts. Look in the fixed-price Lim's in Holland Village, then move on to bargaining in Chinatown and Arab Street. Basketry, wood carvings, Chinese pottery, embroidered silks, wedding baskets, tiffin carriers, cooking utensils and wooden craft items from Bali are all worth looking for.

Electronics can be found in Sim Lim Square and Sim Lim Tower in Bencoolen Street, cameras in Orchard Road and computers in

SHOPPING

the Funan Centre in North Bridge Road. Be aware of the price of the item at home and in the local department stores, check guarantees are international and watch your goods being packed. You don't want any nasty surprises when you get home.

The tourist board produces a free shopping guide, and don't forget that you can claim back the Goods and Services Tax (GST) for purchases over S$100 if the retailer displays a Global Refund Tax Free Shopping sign (W www.globalrefund.com).

❗ Most shops and department stores open daily from around 09.30/10.00–21.00/21.30.

🔺 *Beautiful pottery, and much more, to choose from*

MAKING THE MOST OF SINGAPORE

Eating & drinking

Singaporeans are passionate about food and eat it at every opportunity, whether at plastic tables in hawker centres (see page 28) or in high class restaurants in posh hotels. In Singapore there is a place to eat for every budget, occasion and palate.

Japanese, Thai, European, Korean, Asian fusion, Californian – all the world's cuisines are represented here, but the real eating adventure is to go native and try the local food.

The Singaporean version of Cantonese cooking is characterised by quickly stir fried, bite-sized pieces of food served with a ready-made thickened sauce, often laced with chilli so that sweet and sour sauce takes on a third dimension of hot.

Next in popularity is Szechuan cooking – stir fried combinations with contrasting textures, sesame flavoured, with no accompanying sauce but often served with a giant chilli on the plate.

Chinese haute cuisine is Beijing-style food, blander and based on wheat noodles rather than rice. It's most commonly encountered in expensive restaurants.

Malay food can be found at the hawker places at Geylang and around Arab Street. Typical Malay food is known as *nasi padang* – a plate of rice to which you add your choice from a selection of

> **PRICE CATEGORIES**
> Price ratings in this book are based on the average price of a three-course meal without drinks.
> £ up to S$25   ££ S$25–75   £££ over S$75

EATING & DRINKING

⬤ *At Siem Reap II you can watch the river go by*

MAKING THE MOST OF SINGAPORE

very spicy, often coconut- and lemon grass-flavoured, curries.

Indian restaurants are mostly inexpensive places serving small dollops of rice, flatbreads and curries on banana leaves

HAWKER CENTRES

These places comprise several small kitchen stalls, each serving its own specialities. On arrival, grab a cleared table and park one of your company on it. This can be a cut-throat affair at busy times and, especially at Newton Circus and Lao Pa Sat, tables can be earmarked by one particular stall hoping for a big party of *gweilos* (literally 'white ghosts', a name given to foreigners) with no idea of the cost of their food.

Having established your base roam the stalls, picking whatever you like and giving your table number. The food appears as if by magic, everybody eats and each stallholder retrieves his or her plates. If you order Muslim food, keep those utensils separate.

Dishes to look out for are: satay served with peanut sauce; *laksa* (a glorious soup made with coconut-flavoured curry sauce, rice noodles, shellfish and other bits and pieces); *yong tau fu* (another soup dish with stuffed vegetables added); chicken rice (a lovely simple Hainanese dish); chilli crab (an adventure, as you rip the shreds of meat from the exoskeleton); *mee goreng* (an Indian-influenced fried noodle dish); *roti john* (a French roll dipped in beaten egg, stuffed with minced lamb and fried); and *tahu goreng* (deep-fried beancurd, served with salad and peanut sauce).

EATING & DRINKING

⬢ *A sample of typical Singapore cuisine*

(or, more commonly these days, on steel or polystyrene trays). Muslim Indian curry houses serve a wonderful snack called *roti prata* – a crispy pancake often filled with meat or vegetables (when it becomes a *murtabak*) and accompanied by a fiery curry sauce. For breakfast there are other pancakes or breads; *paratha* is worth seeking out in Serangoon Road or *masala dosa* (rice and gram flour pancakes filled with potatoes and served with coconut sauce).

The best fun, though, is to try Singaporean cuisine served in a hawker centre (see opposite).

MAKING THE MOST OF SINGAPORE

Entertainment & nightlife

Singapore has a thriving nightlife centred around the downtown riverside where the vast interiors of once crumbling and deserted *godowns* (warehouses) have been turned into huge clubs, bars and restaurants. Clarke Quay is where the hip crowd go to quaff champagne cocktails in upmarket joints like **Le Noir** (ⓐ Clarke Quay, 3C River Valley Rd ⓣ 6339 6365) before hitting the glitzy tiles at **Zirca Mega Club** (ⓐ Block C, The Cannery, Clarke Quay ⓣ 6235 2292) and the **Bellini Grande** (ⓐ The Foundry, 3B River Valley Rd ⓣ 6336 7676).

ENTERTAINMENT & NIGHTLIFE

Boat Quay is slightly more run-down, but then this is Singapore we are talking about. The touristy restaurants along the waterfront are best avoided. Instead, try wandering down Circular Road, just behind Boat Quay, where various Irish bars and occasional jazz performances keep things lively. Across the water, Empress Place is a good spot for a laidback drink.

Another area to check out is Dempsey Hill, a former army barracks that has been converted into a hive of humming nightspots. Chijmes (see page 89) is a rather more sedate place where the entertainment continues till late. Further afield,

◆ *Clarke Quay, centre of Singaporean nightlife*

MAKING THE MOST OF SINGAPORE

Rochester Park is a picturesque collection of colonial black-and-white bungalows that are now trendy bars and restaurants.

Alcohol is expensive and prices tend to go up as the venue gets classier. One way to avoid spending wads of cash is to imbibe during 'happy hours', when drinks are either half price or two for one.

There is often a ladies' night midweek, when drinks or the admission charge are free for females.

Live music does quite well in Singapore. For the really big names Singapore Indoor Stadium (see page 22) comes into play. For jazz enthusiasts **Jazz@Southbridge** (ⓐ 82B Boat Quay ⓘ 6327 4671) is almost a Singaporean institution, as is **Harry's Bar** (ⓐ 28 Boat Quay ⓘ 6538 3029). The **Lobby Lounge** at the Intercontinental (ⓐ 80 Middle Rd ⓘ 6338 7600) has a smoochy kind of jazz, while the **Crazy Elephant** (ⓐ 3E River Valley Rd ⓘ 6337 7859), among others at Clarke Quay, has a resident rock band, and **Rouge**, at Peranakan Place, offers live alternative rock.

Going to the movies is a much appreciated form of entertainment in Singapore. Theatres show a range of films in different languages, from Cantonese and Malay to Tamil, all subtitled in English, and western, Hollywood films subtitled in all three languages, which can occasionally interfere with events on the screen.

Alliance Francaise Theatre (ⓐ 1 Sarkies Rd ⓘ 6737 8422) shows weekly films in French, and **Sinema Old School** (ⓐ 11B Mount Sophia ⓘ 6336 9707 ⓦ www.sinema.sg/oldschool) screens interesting local films. For listings of what's on, check out the free monthly magazine *Where*, available from hotel lobbies, tourist offices and other public places. For advance ticket

ENTERTAINMENT & NIGHTLIFE

> **AFTER HOURS**
> Bars now close between 02.00 and 03.00, and clubs between 04.00 and 06.00. At this point most Singaporeans head off for some food or an early breakfast. Hawker centres are the best for this. Newton and Lau Pa Sat in Shenton Way stay open 24 hours, as does the café in the Hyatt Hotel.

bookings contact either **SISTIC** (❶ 6348 5555 ⓦ www.sistic.com) or **Ticketcharge** (❶ 6296 2929 ⓦ www.ticketcharge.com.sg).

❶ Cinema seats are very cold, inexpensive and very popular, so you should bring an extra layer, get your tickets in advance and be there early. Be prepared for the locals chatting throughout the movie. Singaporeans also enjoy snacks while viewing, so expect the sound of popcorn crunching.

MAKING THE MOST OF SINGAPORE

Sport & relaxation

With acres of water, an indecent number of golf courses and swimming pools, inexpensive squash courts, and miles of cycle and rollerblade-friendly paths, Singapore offers lots of opportunities for burning off all that hawker food.

SPECTATOR SPORTS
Cricket
Singapore Cricket Club Entry to the club is members only but you can watch matches from the Padang (🕒 Sat pm & Sun am Mar–Oct).

Football
Twelve teams play in the so-called S. League over the eight months of the football season. International games are for the moment played at the **National Stadium** (ⓐ Kallang 🕒 09.00–17.00 Mon–Fri), though there are vague plans to construct a shiny new national sports stadium if red tape can be sufficiently unravelled.

Horse racing
Singapore Turf Club ⓐ 1 Turf Club Ave ⓣ 6879 1000
ⓦ www.turfclub.com.sg

PARTICIPATION SPORTS
Cycling
Beach Cabana ⓐ East Coast Park Area C ⓣ 6443 3489
🕒 09.00–17.00 Mon–Fri, 08.00–20.00 Sat, Sun & public holidays
Bike & Hike ⓐ 382 Upper Bukit Timah Rd ⓣ 6763 8382

SPORT & RELAXATION

Comfort Rental ⓐ 18 Pulau Ubin ⓣ 6542 0557
ⓦ www.avipclub.com.sg/comfort ⓒ 08.00–18.00

Golf
Changi Golf Club ⓐ 20 Netheravon Rd ⓣ 6545 5133

▲ *Retreat to a spa for some real relaxation*

MAKING THE MOST OF SINGAPORE

Jurong Country Club ⓐ 9 Science Centre Rd ⓣ 6568 5188
Sentosa Gold Club ⓐ 27 Bukit Manis Rd ⓣ 6275 0022

Reverse bungee jumping
GMax Reverse Bungee Jump ⓐ 3E River Valley Rd, Clarke Quay
ⓣ 6338 1146 ⓦ www.gmax.co.nz ⓛ 15.00–01.00 Mon–Thur,
15.00–04.00 Fri, 13.00–04.00 Sat, 13.00–01.00 Sun

Swimming
Buona Vista Swimming Complex ⓐ 76 Holland Dr ⓣ 6778 0244
ⓛ 08.00–21.30
Delta Swimming Complex ⓐ 900 Tiong Bahru Rd ⓣ 6474 7573
ⓛ 08.00–21.30

Water skiing & wakeboarding
Extreme Sports & Marketing ⓐ Kallang Riverside Park
ⓣ 6344 8813 ⓦ www.extreme.com.sg ⓘ By reservation only

Windsurfing
People's Association Water-Venture ⓐ 9 Stadium Link ⓣ 6340 5335
ⓦ www.water-venture.org.sg ⓛ 09.00–18.00 Tues–Sun

RELAXATION
Spas
The Retreat Spa & Thalasso Centre ⓐ Changi Village Hotel,
1 Netheravon Rd ⓣ 6738 0080 ⓦ www.theretreat.com.sg
Spa-lon ⓐ Chijmes ⓣ 6837 0131 ⓦ www.thespa-lon.com
Spa Valley ⓐ 02-02 Cairnhill Place ⓣ 6738 0889
ⓦ www.spavalley.com ⓛ 10.00–19.00

Accommodation

Singapore offers a wide range of places to stay, from the basic to the super-indulgent, according to your needs and your pocket. Little India and the Arab Street area is the centre for budget accommodation. Here you will find hostels with private single and double rooms as well as dorm beds. It's a good place for socialising with fellow travellers and gathering information on the whole Asian travel scene.

HOTELS

Hotel 1929 ££ A good mid-range hotel in the heart of Chinatown. ⓐ 50 Keong Saik Rd (Boat Quay & Chinatown) ⓣ 6347 1929 ⓦ www.hotel1929.com Ⓜ MRT: Chinatown

Perak Hotel ££ A 35-room hotel close to Little India occupying a restored Chinese shop-house; fridge and tea/coffee maker in rooms. ⓐ 12 Perak Rd (Little India & Arab Street) ⓣ 6299 7733 ⓦ www.peraklodge.net Ⓜ MRT: Bugis or Little India

Swissôtel Merchant Court ££ More than 475 comfortable rooms, good food and beverage outlets and an in-house spa. Conveniently

> **PRICE CATEGORIES**
> The ratings in this book indicate the approximate cost of a room for two people for one night, including tax and breakfast.
> **£** up to S$75   **££** S$75–200   **£££** over S$200

located for the city centre and Chinatown. ⓐ 20 Merchant Rd (Boat Quay & Chinatown) ⓘ 6337 2288 ⓦ singapore-merchantcourt.swissotel.com Ⓜ MRT: Clarke Quay

New Majestic £££ Each of the 30 rooms is individually designed, hence the variation in room prices, but expect something bold and arty. There's a good Cantonese restaurant on the premises. ⓐ 31 Bukit Pasoh Rd (Boat Quay & Chinatown) ⓘ 6222 3377 ⓦ www.newmajestichotel.com Ⓜ MRT: Outram Park

The Ritz-Carlton Millenia £££ For pampering, attentive service and sheer indulgence of the senses, no hotel in Singapore is equal to The Ritz-Carlton. The public artwork is outstanding. ⓐ 7 Raffles Ave (Orchard Road & Colonial District) ⓘ 6337 8888 ⓦ www.ritzcarlton.com Ⓜ MRT: City Hall

The Scarlet £££ In Chinatown, this boutique hotel has sex appeal as well as two good restaurants, a relaxing bar, a gym and an outdoor whirlpool. ⓐ 33 Erskine Rd (Boat Quay

HOTEL 81s
Dotted around Singapore are a group of hotels called Hotel 81. These offer the best deals in terms of quality budget accommodation. Prices vary according to location, which includes central areas like Chinatown and Bugis, and to the type of bedroom. Well worth checking out the website ⓦ www.hotel81.com.sg

ACCOMMODATION

The modern and arty lobby of the New Majestic

MAKING THE MOST OF SINGAPORE

● *Luxury at The Ritz-Carlton Millenia*

ACCOMMODATION

& Chinatown) ❶ 6511 3333 ❢ www.thescarlethotel.com
❢ MRT: Chinatown

HOSTELS
Betel Box Backpacker Hostel £ No-frills but reliable and has cheap and excellent public transport connections into town. Also provides free guided tours around town ranging from nature walks to pub crawls. ❢ 200 Joo Chiat Rd (Boat Quay & Chinatown) ❶ 6247 7340 ❢ www.betelbox.com
❢ MRT: Bukit Timah, Changi & Bintan

The Inncrowd £ Backpacker's hostel in the heart of Little India with all the amenities you would expect. If full, try the **Fragrance Backpackers Hostel** (❢ www.fragrancebackpackers.com.sg) next door. ❢ 73 Dunlop St (Little India & Arab Street) ❶ 6296 6169
❢ www.the-inncrowd.com ❢ MRT: Bugis or Little India

Sleepy Sam's £ Good location in a pedestrianised street near Arab Street, with mixed and female-only dorms, private single and double rooms, free internet, kitchen and safe deposit.
❢ 55 Bussorah St (Little India & Arab Street) ❶ 9277 4988
❢ www.sleepysams.com ❢ MRT: Bugis

hangout@mt.emily ££ Hip and affordable with deckchairs on the rooftop, washing machines and dryers, baggage storage, free broadband, private en suite bedrooms and shared rooms, plus air-conditioning. Good deal all round. ❢ 10A Upper Wilkie Rd (Little India & Arab Street) ❶ 6438 5588 ❢ www.hangouthotels.com
❢ MRT: Little India

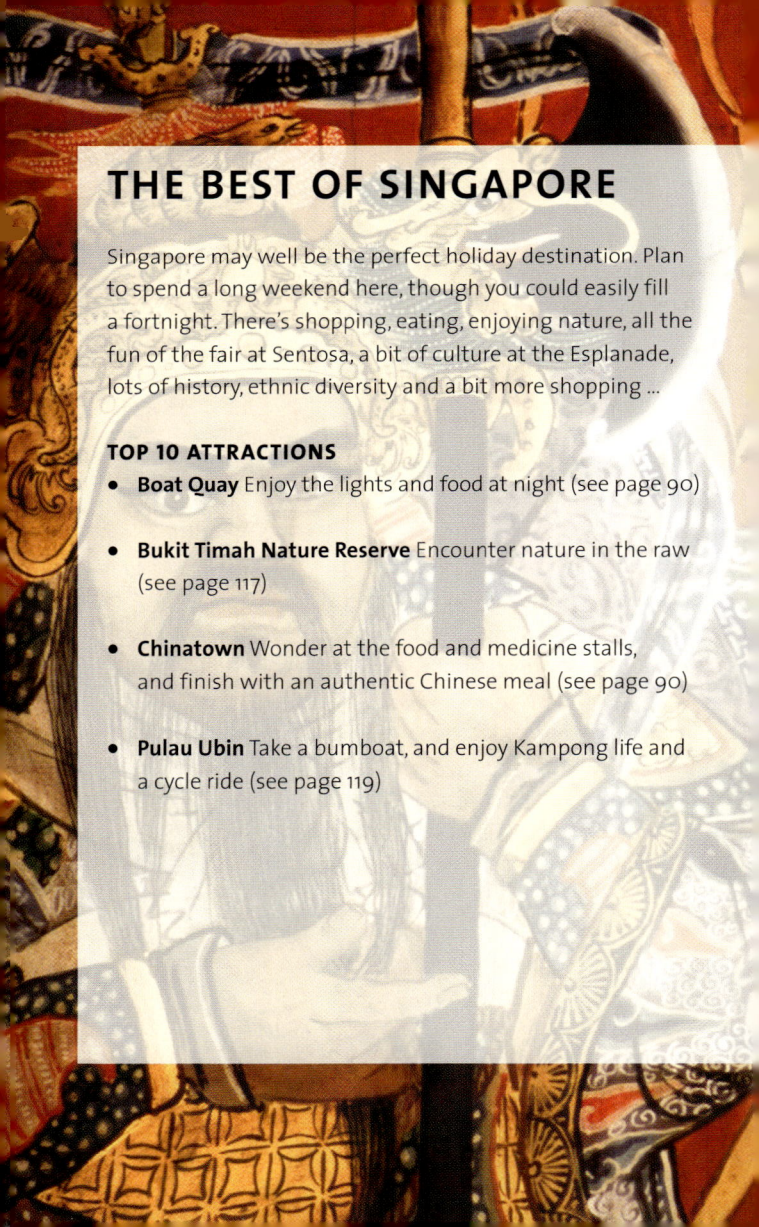

THE BEST OF SINGAPORE

Singapore may well be the perfect holiday destination. Plan to spend a long weekend here, though you could easily fill a fortnight. There's shopping, eating, enjoying nature, all the fun of the fair at Sentosa, a bit of culture at the Esplanade, lots of history, ethnic diversity and a bit more shopping …

TOP 10 ATTRACTIONS

- **Boat Quay** Enjoy the lights and food at night (see page 90)

- **Bukit Timah Nature Reserve** Encounter nature in the raw (see page 117)

- **Chinatown** Wonder at the food and medicine stalls, and finish with an authentic Chinese meal (see page 90)

- **Pulau Ubin** Take a bumboat, and enjoy Kampong life and a cycle ride (see page 119)

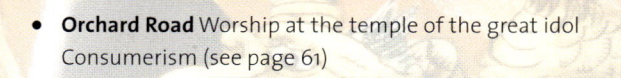

- **Orchard Road** Worship at the temple of the great idol Consumerism (see page 61)

- **Esplanade – Theatres on the Bay ('the durian')** Take in some culture here (see page 60)

- **Sentosa** Relive your childhood at this magical island (see page 109)

- **Serangoon Road** Experience some real-life Singapore (see page 77)

- **Raffles Hotel** Treat yourself to a Singapore Sling cocktail at this famous hotel (see page 64)

- **Thian Hock Keng Temple** Admire the delft roof tiles and ornate decorations (see page 99)

Thian Hock Keng Temple door

MAKING THE MOST OF SINGAPORE

Suggested itineraries

HALF-DAY: SINGAPORE IN A HURRY

With just half a day, Orchard Road is the place for you. It sums up what Singapore is all about and contains some of its most in-your-face architecture. Start at Orchard MRT station, enjoy the wonders of Tang's with its comfortable floors of everything you ever wanted, and then move on through Lucky Plaza where you will see cut-throat selling at work. Work your way down to the recently renovated National Museum in Stamford Road and catch the exhibitions on food and shopping as well as some history. Try to make time for Raffles: *the* spot to relax and enjoy a Singapore Sling.

1 DAY: TIME TO SEE A LITTLE MORE

Plan a day to take in Fort Canning Hill and the Battle Box. Wander round to the Asian Civilisations Museum and wind up at Clarke Quay in the evening, enjoying the brou-ha-ha of Singaporeans letting it all hang out. Round off the day with a trip to Zouk (see page 102).

2–3 DAYS: TIME TO SEE MUCH MORE

Spend one early morning in the Botanic Gardens and the orchid garden, but also look out for groups of people practising tai chi. Make your way to Chinatown in the afternoon for more shopping. Take in the Thian Hock Keng Temple and check out the wet market, where some unusual things are waiting to become someone's dinner. Stay in Chinatown for the evening; the night market in Smith Street offers lots of Chinese delicacies for your evening meal. Another early start could bring you to Singapore Zoo to enjoy breakfast with the animals. Midday, head back to Bukit Timah, pick up a picnic lunch, and head off to Bukit Timah Hill – a wonderful relic of what Singapore was like before civilisation hit it. In the evening Serangoon Road beckons, its shops and restaurants booming with Indian music and the temples alive with activity. Try a banana leaf dinner at one of the many restaurants.

LONGER: ENJOYING SINGAPORE TO THE FULL

With more time on your hands you can fit in a whole day at Sentosa, another day out at Changi and on to Pulau Ubin, a trip out to Jurong and some shopping around Arab Street. Split your evenings between the Esplanade on the Bay, Boat Quay and some of the lively hawker centres such as Lau Pa Sat, Maxwell Street or Newton Circus.

Boat Quay at night

MAKING THE MOST OF SINGAPORE

Something for nothing

Just the expression 'something for nothing' would put many of Singapore's merchants into a state of apoplexy. That said, there are things to do here that won't cost you a cent.

Clearly, window shopping has to be the most entertaining activity and has the advantage of being largely inside so there is the added blessing of free air-conditioning.

There are hours of fun to be had at the Botanic Gardens (see page 105) and at Fort Canning Hill (see page 60) (including several free performances through the summer months), while at Bukit Timah Nature Reserve (see page 117) and Sungei Buloh Wetland Reserve (see page 132, free admission weekdays only) you can see animals every bit as exotic as some of those in the zoo.

At **MacRitchie Reservoir Park** (w www.nparks.gov.sg ● 09.00–17.00 Tues–Fri, 08.30–17.00 Sat & Sun ● Bus: 74, 93, 130, 132) is a treetop walk, suspended 25 m (82 ft) in the air and part of a longer nature walk.

At the Esplanade (see page 60) there are regular free performances in the open air theatre and in the walkways around the theatres. A few museums are free, too. One is the museum in Raffles Hotel (see page 64); so far no one has put an entrance charge on the hotel!

Entrance is also free to the **NUS Museum** (a 50 Kent Ridge Crescent ● 6516 4616 w www.nus.edu.sg/museum ● 10.00–19.30 Tues–Sat, 10.00–18.00 Sun ● MRT: Clementi; Bus: 33, 96, 151, 188), which holds collections of Chinese art, calligraphy and sculpture.

Out of town at Changi (see page 118), the Changi chapel and museum are free, as is the Johor Battery, a World War II gun

SOMETHING FOR NOTHING

▲ *Wander around Bukit Timah Nature Reserve for free*

emplacement, rediscovered a decade or so ago. Here too are beaches and long shady walks along the promenades, where there are free barbecue pits and benches for a picnic. For the cost of your S$2 admission to Sentosa there are still some wildlife areas on the island, while the dancing musical fountain is a little whimsical but free to all.

Finally, if you are transiting through Changi Airport with 5 hours plus, look out for the Free Tour Desks and sign up for the quick coach tour of the city which includes a traditional bumboat ride.

MAKING THE MOST OF SINGAPORE

When it rains

When it rains in Singapore there is absolutely nothing to be done outside. Singaporean rain is scary in its intensity: vision is reduced to a few feet, storm drains fill and roar in a matter of

● *When it rains, try a spot of indoor shopping*

minutes, and everyone runs for the nearest shelter – preferably not a tree on account of the accompanying lightning. Bridges over the motorway fill up with moped riders sheltering from the deluge, and shopping centres fill even fuller. The good news is that most downpours last only 30 minutes or so and the resulting coolness is worth the wait.

If you experience one of the few days when the rain just won't go away there are the museums you can visit: the Battle Box, the National Museum, the Asian Civilisations Museum and Raffles Museum (with the added advantage of Singapore Slings while you wait to go out again).

The shopping malls along Orchard Road, linked with a few dashes in the open, could take a week to seriously explore. Along some of the older shopping streets, such as Arab Street, the covered footpaths (known as 'five foot ways') offer a dry route from shop to shop.

The cinema is a joy in Singapore. You could try a Cantonese movie subtitled in English, or even a Hindi or Malay movie with their abrupt shifts from violence to song and dance.

One of Singapore's covered wetmarkets is an education in food tastes and can offer a good 30 minutes of fascinating study of the things that people consider food. Most wetmarkets have hawker centres attached where you can try some local delicacies.

Considering the briefness of Singapore's showers and the fact that most of them seem to start around lunchtime, an hour in a restaurant is also an enjoyable occupation. Or if you can find shelter outside – such as the five foot ways or a shop doorway – just watching the vast amounts of water falling out of the sky can be quite entertaining, too.

MAKING THE MOST OF SINGAPORE

On arrival

TIME DIFFERENCE
Singapore is eight hours ahead of the UK.

ARRIVING
By air
You cannot fail to be impressed by Changi Airport, which is like a little city and could survive entirely on its own even if all the rest of the island disappeared. Facilities at the airport include shopping centres, hotels, free sleeping areas, showers, a free trip around town for transit passengers, cinemas, wireless internet

▲ *The bus system in Singapore is well run*

connection, games areas, several food courts, post offices, money exchange, banks and left luggage.

The airport is linked to the city centre by MRT, bus and several taxi options, as well as a city shuttle. The MRT links terminals 2 and 3 with the city. Fares are S$1.70 and the journey takes 40 minutes or so. An alternative is to take a maxicab; these leave every 15 minutes and will take you, along with other passengers, to your hotel. The most expensive option is a regular taxi, which will cost around S$20.

By rail

Trains from Malaysia and Thailand arrive at Tanjong Pagar Railway Station, where you will encounter passport control and some sniffer dogs. A cab or bus 97 will bring you into town. Cabs are metered.

By road

Buses from Malaysia and Thailand come directly into the city to Lavender Street Coach Terminal or the Johor Bahru Bus Depot on Queen Street, depending on the bus company. Both terminals are in the city centre and close to MRT stations.

There really is very little reason to drive in Singapore. Parking is expensive and tolls are levied every time you enter the restricted areas during business hours. Add to this traffic jams and a surcharge for travelling into Malaysia, and the thought of the traffic-free MRT sounds better every minute.

FINDING YOUR FEET

The first bit of acclimatising is to slow down! The place is

MAKING THE MOST OF SINGAPORE

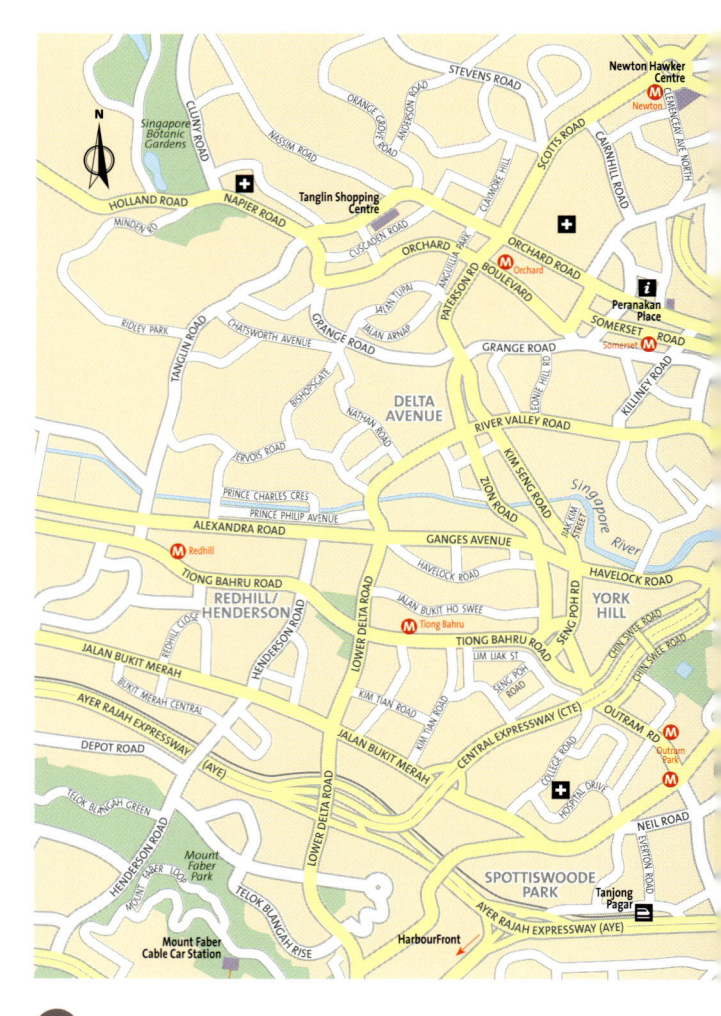

ON ARRIVAL

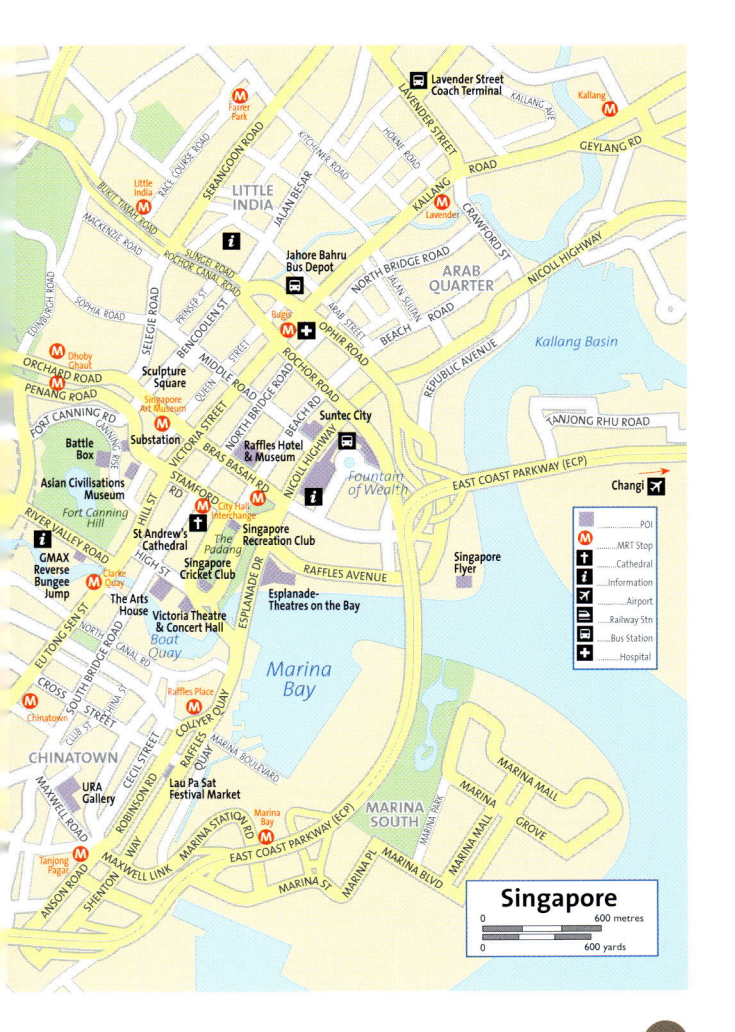

Singapore

MAKING THE MOST OF SINGAPORE

seriously hot so energetic walking will exhaust you. Singaporeans know their way around town via air-conditioned routes, shady pathways and the MRT, and the wise tourist will follow their example. Once you have learned to spot a good bit of shade and bought an umbrella (twofold usage: shade in desperation and keeping off the rain while you run for shelter), it's time to realise that this is a fine country. There are fines for most things you take for granted – especially jaywalking and snacking on the MRT.

Traffic, like everything else in Singapore, obeys the rules, so no speeding cars but also no slowing down for wandering pedestrians. Crime is not a big issue, but it is as well to follow the rules of any big city – avoid parks alone late at night, keep your belongings safe in your hotel room and be aware of where your handbag/wallet is at all times. Pickpockets operate in crowded areas and especially love backpacks and people with buggies – they are easy to distract. You must remember to drink more (water!) and use sunscreen.

ORIENTATION

Singapore is a tiny city state. Most of the sights, hotels, restaurants and shopping centres are located close together, which is fortunate since the heat can be overpowering.

The river forms the heart of the city, flowing roughly east–west across the island, with both of its banks filled with bars, clubs and restaurants, replacing the old commercial port of Singapore. To the north and running vaguely parallel is Orchard Road and between them lies the financial district. North again are Little India and the Arab Quarter. Immediately south of the river is Chinatown.

ON ARRIVAL

Beyond these central areas lay satellite towns. To the east is Changi and the tiny island of Pulau Ubin; to the far west is Jurong with the Bird Park and Sentosa; and to the north, Sungei Buloh and the wild lands of Woodlands and Johor Bahru.

If you get lost, everyone speaks English (or anyway, Singlish) and will be pleased to put you right.

The tourist board hands out maps of the island, which will be all you need to navigate your way around.

GETTING AROUND

Considerable thought has to be given to getting around Singapore. Just 10 minutes' walk can make children ratty and ruin a linen outfit.

Public transport

The MRT is a godsend. Its five lines – North South, North East, East West, Circle (with line extensions under construction) and Downtown (also under construction) – cover most tourist destinations. Trains run from 05.30–00.30 and fares begin at 90 cents. Single fares can be bought at machines in each station or you can buy an ez-link card, which (like the British Oyster card) is rechargeable and valid on buses too. For a S$5 refundable deposit you can buy a card in MRT stations with a minimum value of S$10, which is convenient and makes journeys slightly cheaper. Do not eat or drink, smoke or carry *durians* (a popular fruit) on the MRT.

The bus network covers the entire island and if you are a bus enthusiast you can make every journey that way. Fares start at 70 cents and you must have the exact fare. You can use the

MAKING THE MOST OF SINGAPORE

A Communicarta
Style45 design
© Communicarta Ltd 2009 UDN.6
Map user Ref: WZFG/CS/SIN/2009/96
Malaysia
Selat Johor
Yishun
Khatib
Yio Chu Kang
Ang Mo Kio
Bishan
Braddell
Toa Payoh
Serangoon
Novena
Newton
Orchard
Somerset
Dhoby Ghaut
Clarke Quay
Chinatown
City Hall
Raffles Place
Tanjong Pagar
Marina Bay
5
Keppel Harbour
Thanggam
Fernvale
Layar
Tongkang
Renjong
Kupang
Farmway
Cheng Lim
7
Punggol
Oasis
Cove
Kadaloor
Meridian
Coral Edge
Riviera
Sengkang
Compassvale
Rumbia
Ranggung
Bakau
Kangkar
Buangkok
Hougang
Kovan
Lorong Chuan
Serangoon
Potong Pasir
Boon Keng
Farrer Park
Little India
Bartley
8
Tai Seng
MacPherson
Tampines
401
Kallang
Aljunied
Paya Lebar
Lavender
Bugis
Bras Basah
Esplanade
Dakota
Mountbatten
Stadium
Nicoll Highway
Promenade
Bayfront
2
29
Changi Village Terminal
Serangoon Harbour
Pasir Ris
1
3
Changi Airport
Tampines
Simei
Expo
Tanah Merah
401
Bedok
Kembangan
Eunos
35
Tanah Merah Ferry Terminal
401
Bintan Island
Straits of Singapore
Bedok Route terminus station
1 Destination or Route Number
Interchange station
Please note that station names on the Circle and Downtown lines currently under construction are subject to change

ez-link card on buses. Some buses are not air-conditioned.

There are several tourist-orientated buses running from one sight to another. The SIA hop-on hop-off bus runs from Orchard Road, Suntec City, Clarke Quay and Marina Bay. Another route travels to Sentosa. You can buy a day pass for S$12. Alternatively, if you have flown in on Singapore Airlines, use of the buses is free.

Taxis

Compared to Europe these are inexpensive and abundant – and also another method of heat avoidance. They are metered, so you don't have to worry about negotiating fares, and many of them have credit card machines. Fares start at S$2.80, and there are extra charges for use of the boot, journeys after midnight, booking in advance, passing into the Electronic Road Pricing (ERP) area and pick up from the airport. If your taxi starts to 'bing' at regular intervals, the driver is speeding. Cabs have a built-in speed limit monitor.

CAR HIRE

If you need to hire a car, you are required to show proof of identification and your driving licence. You must also buy a stored value cash card to drive into the ERP area and parking coupons which can be bought at booths close to car parks and 7–Eleven stores.

Avis ⓐ Terminal 2, Changi Airport ⓣ 6542 8855 ⓒ 07.00–23.00
Hertz ⓐ Terminals 2 & 3, Changi Airport ⓣ 6542 5300
ⓒ 07.00–23.00

▶ *Singapore's biggest mosque – Sultan Mosque*

THE CITY OF
Singapore

THE CITY

Orchard Road & Colonial District

The historical, emotional and cultural heart of the city, this area is where you will spend most of your time when it comes to shopping, exploring museums and finding good places to eat.

SIGHTS & ATTRACTIONS

Esplanade – Theatres on the Bay
Nicknamed by locals 'the durian' on account of the complex's spiky appearance, this gobsmacking site occupies 6 hectares (15 acres) of reclaimed land and includes a concert hall, theatre, two performance studios, two outdoor theatre spaces, lots of – surprise! – F&B (food and beverage) outlets and a shopping mall. ⓐ 1 Esplanade Dr ⓘ 6828 8377 (general); 6348 5555 (tickets) ⓦ www.esplanade.com ⓛ 10.00–22.00; guided tours: 11.00 & 14.00 Mon–Fri ⓜ MRT: City Hall; Bus: 36, 56, 75, 77, 97, 106, 111, 133, 162, 171, 174M, 195, 700A. Admission charge for theatre performances

Fort Canning Hill
Somehow, amid this concrete jungle of a city, this little park has survived. Right behind the commercial hubbub of Orchard Road, orioles sing, cicadas chirrup and all manner of unregulated creatures lurk. The 19th-century gravestones of the early white folk have been relocated to the park walls, the crumbling army buildings given a new lease of life in the form of an arts and cooking (what else?) academy, and F&B outlets and Raffles' botanic garden and lighthouse have been born again. ⓐ Fort Canning Hill, entrances at Hill St, Canning Rise, Percival Rd, River

ORCHARD ROAD & COLONIAL DISTRICT

Valley Rd, Canning Walk ❶ 6332 1200 ❿ www.nparks.gov.sg
❿ MRT: Dhoby Ghaut, Clarke Quay; Bus to Penang Rd: 7, 14, 16, 36, 64, 65, 77, 106, 111, 124, 162, 167, 171, 174

Orchard Road
Possibly the world's most densely packed shopping street, Orchard Road is a mile of consumerism deified. While once-great architects built huge edifices in praise of an omnipresent, omnipotent and divine being, in this street all that genius, beauty, glass and granite has gone into retail. Look on their works ye mighty and despair. ❿ MRT: Orchard, Somerset

◯ *Esplanade – Theatres on the Bay – is on the waterfront overlooking Marine Bay*

THE CITY

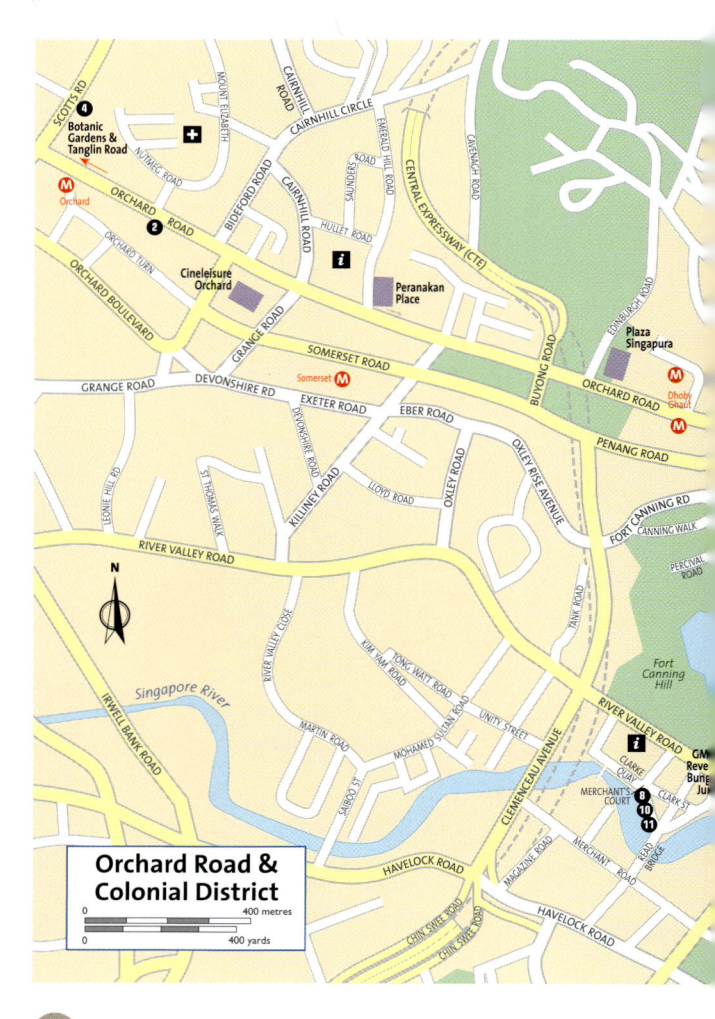

Orchard Road & Colonial District

ORCHARD ROAD & COLONIAL DISTRICT

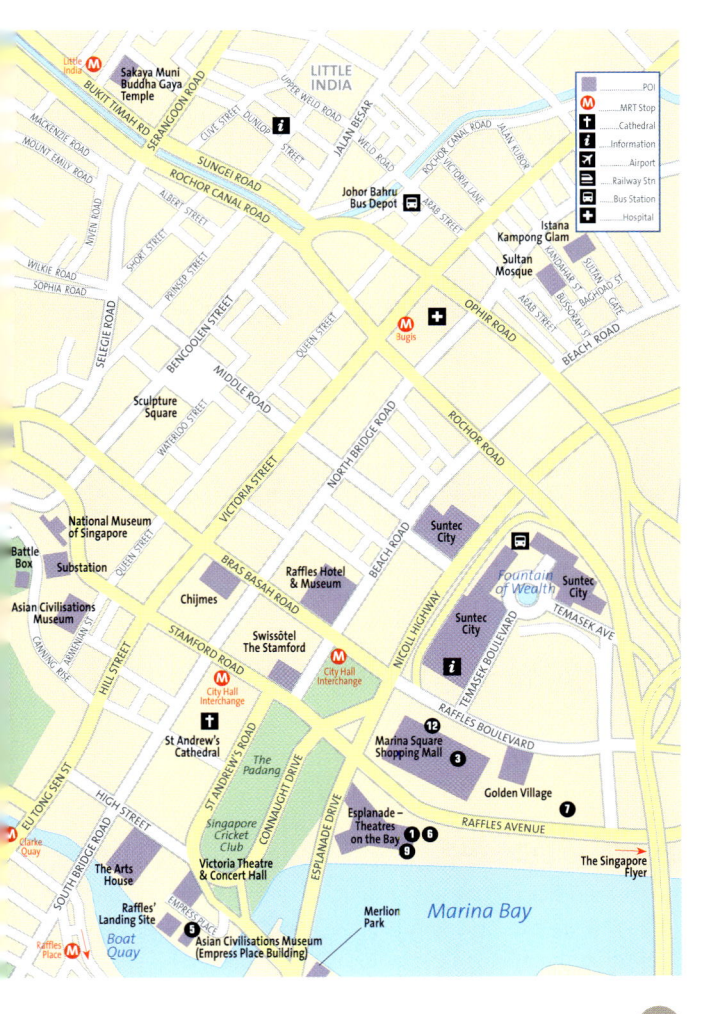

THE CITY

The Padang

The place where once crinolined ladies with powdered hair took their evening stroll, the Padang has been a sport and recreation area since Raffles decided it would be in the early 19th century. In the southeast corner is the Singapore Cricket Club, established for the exclusive use of white men and still very exclusive, while on the other side is the Singapore Recreation Club, set up by the *stengahs*, Singapore's 19th-century mixed race community. MRT: City Hall; Bus: 36, 56, 75, 77, 97, 106, 111, 133, 162, 171, 174M, 195, 700A.

Raffles Hotel

For years in the 20th century a run-down, sleazy kind of place, in 1991 it got the Singapore treatment and is the glossy institution you see before you. The building became an exclusive hotel in the 1880s. A-list celebs started staying here long before Michael Jackson graced its luxury suite – Joseph Conrad, Somerset Maugham, Noel Coward, Rudyard Kipling and many more. The lobby is open to non-paying guests – no riff-raff though. If you don't look well dressed enough you may be asked to leave.
1 Beach Rd 6412 1143 www.raffles.com MRT: City Hall; Bus: 7, 14, 16, 36, 77, 97, 131, 162, 167, 171, 700

Raffles' Landing Site

The place where it is thought that Sir Stamford Raffles, Singapore's founder, might have stepped ashore in 1819 is marked with a marble statue of the man himself. Nice river scenes, and close by are all the delights of Boat Quay and the Asian Civilisations Museum. Boat Quay MRT: Raffles Place; Bus: 70, 82, 97, 100, 107, 130, 131, 162, 167, 196, 700

ORCHARD ROAD & COLONIAL DISTRICT

The Singapore Flyer
Singapore's latest addition to its compelling set of reasons to visit is this bigger, better and classier version of the London Eye, located at the south-east tip of the Marina Centre. It gives great views of the colonial district, the riverside and sparkly skyscrapers, especially at sunset. This being Singapore, there's also a shopping complex with dining outlets and a super-fun **flight simulator experience** (see ⓦ www.flightexperience.com.sg). ⓐ 30 Raffles Ave ⓣ 6333 3311 ⓦ www.singaporeflyer.com ⓞ 08.30–22.30 Ⓜ MRT: City Hall

CULTURE

Asian Civilisations Museum
The ten or so galleries cover Asian cultural life from Islam to China and all stops in between. The best bit is the gallery dedicated to the life of the Singapore River, its banks now a glitzy series of outlets but once the economic heart of the island. A second branch in the restored Tao Nan School in Armenian Street focuses on Chinese and Peranakan culture.
ⓐ 1 Empress Place ⓣ 6332 7798 ⓦ www.acm.org.sg ⓞ 09.00–19.00 Tues–Thur, Sat & Sun, 13.00–19.00 Mon, 09.00–21.00 Fri Ⓜ MRT: City Hall, Raffles Place; Bus: 70, 82, 97, 100, 107, 130, 131, 162, 167, 196, 700. Admission charge (covers both branches)
ⓐ 39 Armenian St ⓣ 6332 3015 ⓦ www.acm.org.sg ⓞ 09.00–19.00 Tues–Thur, Sat & Sun, 13.00–19.00 Mon, 09.00–21.00 Fri Ⓜ MRT: City Hall; Bus: 7, 14, 16, 36, 77, 97, 131, 162, 167, 171, 700. Admission charge (covers both branches)

THE CITY

Battle Box
This series of underground bunkers was the headquarters of the British command during World War II. It was from here that the British decided to surrender to the Japanese. The 26 chambers contain authentic machinery and other items used, and gives a very stark impression of what life must have been like for those cramped in down here with not enough air and the sound of bombs falling overhead. ⓐ 51 Canning Rise ⓘ 6333 0510 ⓒ 10.00–18.00 (closed 1st day of Chinese New Year) ⓜ MRT: Dhoby Ghaut; Bus to Penang Rd: 7, 14, 16, 36, 64, 65, 77, 106, 111, 124, 162, 167, 171, 174. Admission charge

▲ *The National Museum of Singapore is an impressive building*

ORCHARD ROAD & COLONIAL DISTRICT

National Museum of Singapore
Newly reopened after three years of renovations, the museum and its new extension offer a history of the island, exhibitions of contemporary life and much more. ⓐ 93 Stamford Rd
ⓘ 6332 3659 ⓦ www.nationalmuseum.sg ⓛ History Gallery: 10.00–18.00; Living Galleries: 10.00–21.00 ⓝ MRT: Dhoby Ghaut. Admission charge

Raffles Hotel Museum
Full of bits and pieces turned up by locals, such as old photos and maps, plus memorabilia that survived the wilderness years after World War II, the museum is well worth a few minutes' nostalgia for an almost forgotten way of life. ⓐ 1 Beach Rd
ⓘ 6412 1143 ⓦ www.raffles.com ⓛ 10.00–19.00 ⓝ MRT: City Hall; Bus: 7, 14, 16, 36, 77, 97, 131, 162, 167, 171, 700

RETAIL THERAPY

Asian Civilisations Museum Shop Offering quality arts and crafts, museum replicas, fixed prices and a calm atmosphere; the shop can be visited without having to pay to visit the museum.
ⓐ 1 Empress Place ⓘ 6332 7798 ⓦ www.museumshop.com.sg
ⓛ 09.00–19.00 Tues–Thur, Sat & Sun, 13.00–19.00 Mon, 09.00–21.00 Fri ⓝ MRT: City Hall, Raffles Place; Bus: 70, 82, 97, 100, 107, 130, 131, 162, 167, 196, 700

Chapter 2 Hairdressing salon with a reputation for quality cuts but, although the basic deals are reasonably priced, expect to pay a lot for anything special. ⓐ 03-258 Marina

Square, 6 Raffles Blvd ☎ 6338 0112 🌐 www.chapter-2.com
🕐 11.00–22.00 Ⓜ MRT: City Hall

Marina Square Linked to the Marina Mandarin, The Oriental and Pan Pacific hotels, this is a premier shopping mall where bargains are rare. Mostly fashion and lifestyle outlets.
📍 6 Raffles Blvd 🌐 www.marinasquare.com.sg 🕐 10.00–22.00
Ⓜ MRT: City Hall

Orchard Road: Scotts Road to Plaza Singapura The junction of Orchard Road and Scotts Road is dominated by Tangs, one of the best all-purpose department stores in the city, while on Scotts Road itself Far East Plaza is good for avant-garde fashions from overseas. Lucky Plaza, next to Tangs, has camera and electronics shops but could prove unlucky if you don't already have an idea of a product's price. Wisma Atria, across the road, has affordable fashion and lifestyle outlets (and an inexpensive food hall). Next door, the huge and monstrous-looking Ngee Ann City has a large bookstore and countless shops. Cross the road again and you'll hit The Paragon, which houses Metro, a popular mid-range local department store, and a slew of up-market brands. Opposite, Centrepoint has the reputable Robinsons department store and a myriad of assorted shops. Plaza Singapura has a bit of everything and avoids being outrageously expensive. 🌐 www.fareast-plaza.com, www.centrepoint.com.sg, www.ngeeanncity.com.sg, www.wismaonline.com 🕐 10.00–22.00 Ⓜ MRT: Orchard, Somerset, Dhoby Ghaut

ORCHARD ROAD & COLONIAL DISTRICT

Orchard Road: Tanglin to Scotts Road Tanglin Road, which runs into the bottom end of Orchard Road, has three shopping malls – Tanglin, Tudor Court and Tanglin Place – full of artwork and antique outlets. The Forum, further up on Orchard Road itself, is good for toys and children's clothes. Hilton Shopping Centre, next door, is rather haute couture but for more affordable fashions walk up to Liat Towers and Wheelock Place. ⏱ 10.00–22.00 Ⓜ MRT: Orchard

Planet Traveller Everything for the traveller by way of luggage, accessories and assorted gadgets, plus a useful repair service (closed on Sun) for jammed locks, ripped zips and such like.
📍 03-113 Marina Square Shopping Mall ☎ 6337 0291
🌐 www.planettraveller.com ⏱ 10.30–21.00 Ⓜ MRT: City Hall

Raffles Shop Just about everything here has the Raffles logo, including a set of Royal Doulton chinaware and a Wedgewood plate also that might just be a collector's item someday.
📍 1 Beach Rd ☎ 6412 1143 ⏱ 08.30–21.00 Ⓜ MRT: City Hall; Bus: 7, 14, 16, 36, 77, 97, 131, 162, 167, 171, 700

Royal Selangor Hundreds of pewter items suitable as gifts or for your own home. Factory tours also available; café in the shop. 📍 3A River Valley Rd, Clarke Quay ☎ 6268 9600
🌐 www.royalselangor.com ⏱ 09.00–21.00 Ⓜ MRT: Clarke Quay; Bus: 54 (from Scotts Rd), 32, 195 (from City Hall MRT station)

Suntec City Mall From City Hall MRT station, you run a gauntlet of consumer outlets in the subterranean City Link Mall to reach

THE CITY

Suntec City where more than 1,000 retail stores make this the largest shopping mall in Singapore. There is little use coming here without a healthy set of credit cards but, for the super solvent, this is a consumer's paradise. 🅐 Temasek Blvd 3699 🅣 6268 9600 🅦 www.sunteccity.com.sg 🅛 09.00–22.00 🅝 MRT: City Hall (Exit G, via CityLink Mall)

TAKING A BREAK

Chocz £ ❶ Chocolate fondues, muffins, apple crumble, cakes galore, milk shakes, sodas and coffees. 🅐 02-15 Esplanade Mall 🅣 6238 0803 🅦 www.chocz.com.sg 🅛 11.00–21.00 🅝 MRT: City Hall

Food Republic £ ❷ Probably the best food centre along Orchard Road; come here for Indian, Thai or Chinese. Very busy

THE LEGENDARY LONG BAR
The Long Bar at the Raffles Hotel has been a popular drinking hole since the hotel opened in 1887. If you go there now the only drink you are likely to see being served is the famous, but not exactly addictive, Singapore Sling. This famous cocktail was created by bartender Ngiam Tong Boon in 1915 and an average of 2,000, at S$26 a shot, are sold every day in the hotel's various outlets. 🅐 Raffles Hotel, 1 Beach Rd 🅣 6412 1229 🅛 11.00–00.30 Sun–Thur, 11.00–23.30 Fri & Sat; happy hour 17.00–21.00 Sun–Thur 🅝 MRT: City Hall; Bus: 7, 14, 16, 36, 77, 97, 131, 162, 167, 171 ,700

ORCHARD ROAD & COLONIAL DISTRICT

at lunchtime so get your drink first and leave it on a table to reserve a seat while collecting your food. ⓐ 4th Level, Wisma Atria, Orchard Rd ⓒ 09.00–21.00 Ⓝ MRT: Orchard

Marina Food Loft £ ❸ Sit inside for air-conditioned comfort or outside in the evening under fans and facing the river. Great outlets here, like Thai Delights, Sammy's Curry Restaurant, Buona Pasta and Claypot Rice. ⓐ 4th Level, Marina Square, 6 Raffles Blvd ⓒ 11.00–22.00 Ⓝ MRT: City Hall

Picnic Food Court £ ❹ Mostly Chinese food outlets but also Pastamania and Lerk Thai and, ideal for vegetarians, filling yogurts at Yami. ⓐ Basement Level, Scotts Shopping Centre, Scotts Rd ⓒ 11.00–22.00 Ⓝ MRT: Orchard

Siem Reap II £ ❺ Salads, Western and Asian food, desserts and children's menu. Sit outside facing the river with a cold beer or iced coffee. ⓐ Asian Civilisations Museum, 1 Empress Place ⓣ 6338 7596 Ⓦ www.indochine.com.sg ⓒ 11.00–22.30 Ⓝ MRT: Raffles Place; Bus: 70, 82, 97, 100, 107, 130, 131, 162, 167, 196, 700

The Cookie Museum £–££ ❻ You'll find it hard to resist the sampling trolley full of bite-sized goodies that comes round every so often. The menu is a little on the pricey side for cakes and teas, but everything is immaculately presented and the atmosphere is pure olde worlde. ⓐ 01-02 Esplanade Mall, 8 Raffles Ave ⓣ 6333 1965 ⓒ 12.00–22.00 Ⓝ MRT: City Hall

THE CITY

AFTER DARK

RESTAURANTS

Greenhouse ££ ❼ Never mind the Sunday Champagne brunch, Greenhouse undoubtedly offers the best evening buffet in the city, and on Friday and Saturday nights gourmets meet gourmands at a seafood feast. ⓐ Ritz-Carlton Millenia, Raffles Ave ❶ 6434 5288 ⓦ www.ritzcarlton.com ⓛ 12.00–14.30, 18.30–22.30 ⓜ MRT: City Hall

Madame Butterfly ££ ❽ The menu of southeast Asian dishes can be mixed with the one downstairs from Bar Cocoon (where the fried rice is superior). Check out the arctic-cold vodka cocktail bar. ⓐ Merchant's Court, Clarke Quay ❶ 6557 6266 ⓦ www.indochine.com.sg ⓛ 12.00–15.00, 18.30–23.00 Mon–Sat ⓜ MRT: Clarke Quay; Bus: 54 (from Scotts Rd), 32, 195 (from City Hall MRT station)

My Humble House ££ ❾ Convenient for a meal after a show, with Asian fusion dishes like *laksa* with rock oysters. ⓐ 02-27 Esplanade Mall, 8 Raffles Ave ❶ 6423 1881 ⓦ www.tunglok.com ⓛ 12.00–15.00, 18.30–23.00 ⓜ MRT: City Hall; Bus: 36, 56, 75, 77, 97, 106, 111, 133, 162, 171, 174M, 195, 700A

Peony-Jade Restaurant ££ ❿ Szechuan and Cantonese cuisine in an attractive, plush restaurant occupying a converted *godown*. Start with the soft shell crab or the hot and sour soup served in a Martini glass, before tucking into the smoked duck, or baked lamb or beef in a beer sauce. ⓐ Block 3A, Clarke Quay ❶ 6338 0305

ORCHARD ROAD & COLONIAL DISTRICT

Enjoy an evening buffet at Greenhouse

THE CITY

ⓦ www.peonyjade.com. ⓒ 11.00–15.00, 18.00–23.00 ⓜ MRT: Clarke Quay; Bus: 54 (from Scotts Rd), 32, 195 (from City Hall MRT station)

Quayside Seafood ££ ⓫ Fresh seafood, including live lobster and prawns, and a choice of cooking methods. Reserve a riverside table for the best views. ⓐ Clarke Quay ⓣ 6338 0138 ⓦ www.quaysidedining.com ⓒ 18.00–00.00 Sun–Thur, 18.00–01.00 Fri & Sat ⓜ MRT: Clarke Quay; Bus: 54 (from Scotts Rd), 32, 195 (from City Hall MRT station)

Ristorante Bologna £££ ⓬ Still *the* Italian restaurant in Singapore. Try the parma ham or porcini mushrooms with lobster for starters, while the pappardelle with prawns and saffron sauce competes with fish, lamb and beef dishes as the best choice for main courses. Reserve a table by the window for the sound and sight of a waterfall. Sunday brunch is a feast. ⓐ Marina Mandarin Hotel, Raffles Blvd, Marina Square ⓣ 6845 1111 ⓦ www.meritus-hotels.com ⓒ 12.00–14.30 Mon–Fri, 18.30–22.30 Mon–Sat ⓜ MRT: City Hall

BARS

New Asia Bar This is the highest bar in Singapore, on the 71st floor of the Swissôtel. Stunning views of the city and on a clear night you can see the lights of Malaysia. Not the cheapest drinks in town but certainly the highest. ⓐ Swissôtel, The Stamford, 2 Stamford Rd ⓣ 6431 7095 ⓒ 11.00–00.30 Sun–Thur, 11.00–23.30 Fri & Sat ⓜ MRT: City Hall

CINEMAS, THEATRES & SHOWS

Cineleisure Orchard As well as the cinema complex, there is the e-gaming attraction E2Max@Cine–L9 with more than 160 e-gaming stations. ⓐ 8 Grange Rd ⓣ 6733 5969 ⓦ www.cathaycineleisure.com.sg ⓞ 10.00–22.00 ⓝ MRT: Somerset

Esplanade – Theatres on the Bay Asian and Western theatre, opera, musicals and dance and, every Friday to Sunday night, free outdoor performances. ⓐ 1 Esplanade Dr ⓣ 6828 8377 ⓦ www.esplanade.com ⓞ 10.00–22.00 ⓝ MRT: City Hall

Golden Village Multiscreen cinema complex with a bowling alley next door and snooker tables opposite. ⓐ 3rd Level Marina Square ⓣ 6334 3766 (cinema) ⓦ www.gv.com.sg (cinema, book online) ⓞ 10.00–03.00 (bowling alley) ⓝ MRT: City Hall

THE CITY

Little India & Arab Street

It is probably in this area of Singapore that visitors will come close to an idea of what the tiny city state was like for most of its existence. Serangoon Road especially is about as messy as Singapore gets with its traffic-clogged road, loud temples and small merchants selling traditional Indian goods. The Arab Street area has succumbed a little more to the renovators but still gives a sense of what things used to be like. Wheras most of the city's young people aspire to a condo, credit card and car this area is home to people and sights that are not encompassed by the new Singapore values.

Indians, many of them transported convicts from the British Empire, came to settle in this area around the middle of the 19th century when it contained brick kilns and herds of buffalo (hence some of the street names) and have stayed, with every new wave of immigrants heading for the area.

SIGHTS & ATTRACTIONS

Arab Street

By the time the state got round to renovating Arab Street the developers had learned their lesson and interfered as little as they could with the thriving community while ensuring that it provided maximum tourist interest. Arab Street, like it always has been, is a glorious blaze of colour – fabric shops, perfume shops, basketry, leather goods – perhaps more orientated to the tourist trade than 20 years ago but still occupied by one of Singapore's ethnic minorities. Great for shopping.

LITTLE INDIA & ARAB STREET

Little India Conservation Area
The Little India Conservation Area brings together the best of Indian culture in a tidy kind of way, although there's no substitute for a wander down Serangoon Road on a Sunday night. Here you will find shops and a food centre, you can get your hands hennaed, your fortune told by a parrot or dress up in Indian clothes for a photo opportunity. ⓐ Serangoon Rd
ⓝ MRT: Little India; Bus: 64, 65, 114

Serangoon Road
Once past the tidied up areas at the top of the road, Serangoon quickly resolves into a vibrant, living Indian community. Come

▲ *A typical stall in Little India*

THE CITY

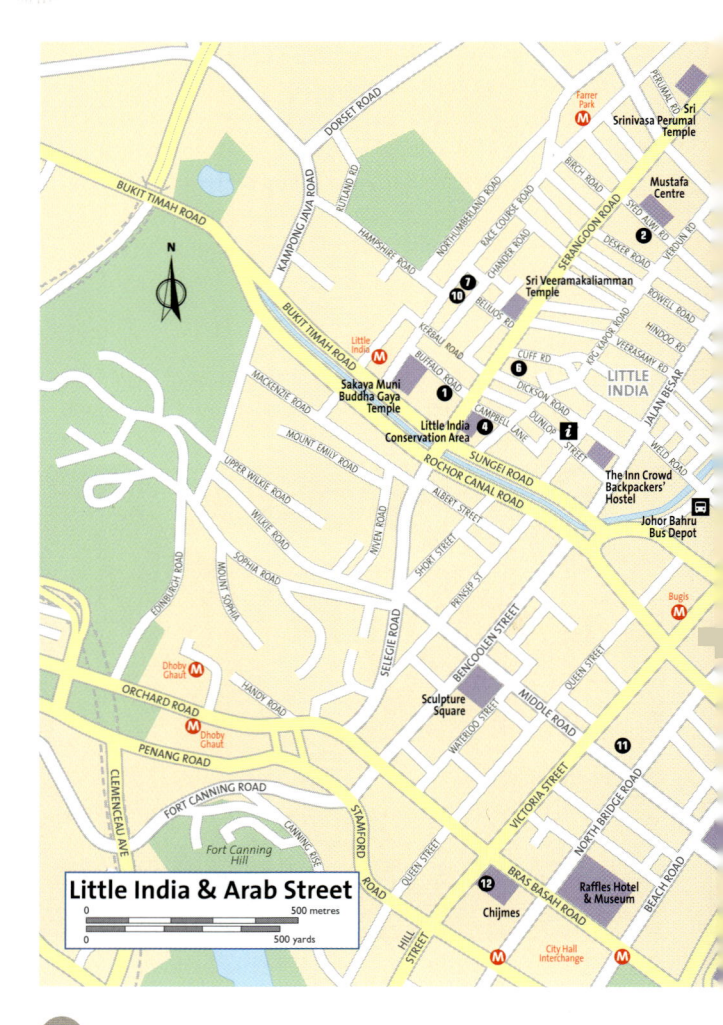

Little India & Arab Street

LITTLE INDIA & ARAB STREET

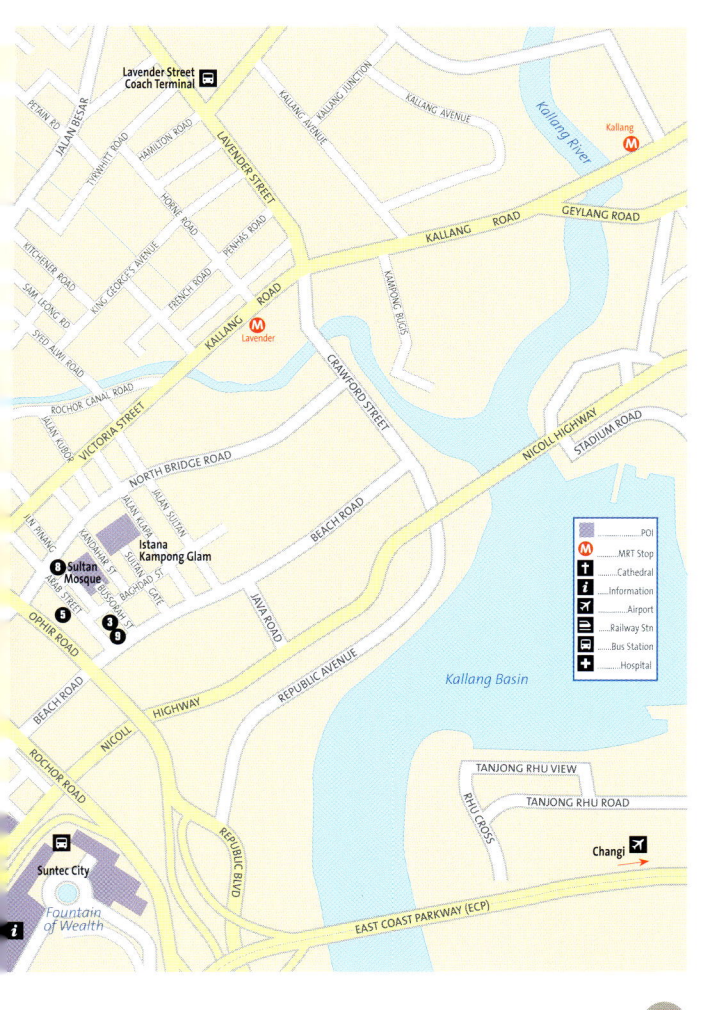

THE CITY

here on Sunday nights when the migrant workers congregate and you could be in the backstreets of Delhi. Indian department stores, spice grinders, garland makers, cheap Indian music CD sellers, gold jewellery and sari shops, the aromatic perfumes emanating from the many cafés, men selling betelnuts, and sex workers peeping out from some of the side streets all make this one of the most unregulated and genuine parts of the island. The people who live, work and worship along this street are remarkably tolerant of the tourists, and there are some amazing restaurants and coffee shops to sample. The most surprising are the fast food places serving tasty authentic food at laughably low prices. ⓐ Serangoon Rd; self guided tours are available from ⓐ 65 Kerbau Rd ⓣ 6329 1772 ⓦ www.spell7.net ⓛ 10.00–16.30 Tues–Sat. There is a charge for hire of headsets ⓜ MRT: Little India; Bus: 64, 65, 114

CULTURE

Istana Kampong Glam

Once the palace of the island's Malay rulers, Kampong Glam has been reclaimed from the crumbling decay of the late 20th century to be a showcase of Malay history and culture on the island. The old colonial house is now a restaurant and in the grounds are exhibits on the Malay film-making industry and a model of a Malay village. Daily cultural shows include Malay dancing, martial arts and music. Pottery making and batik making workshops also take place when there are large enough crowds. ⓐ 85 Sultan Gate ⓣ 6391 0450 ⓦ www.malayheritage.org.sg ⓛ 13.00–18.00 Mon, 10.00–18.00 Tues–Sun; cultural shows:

15.30 Wed ⓝ MRT: Bugis; Bus: 7, 32, 51, 63, 80, 145, 197. Admission charge to exhibitions; entrance to compound is free

Sakaya Muni Buddha Gaya Temple

Better known as the Temple of a Thousand Lights, this strongly Thai influenced Buddhist temple is dominated by a 300 ton, 15 m (49 ft) tall statue of the Lord Buddha. The base of the temple is decorated with scenes from the Buddha's life. Inside the hollow statue is another representation of the Buddha, this one showing the master reclining. Hundreds of electric lights decorate the room, giving the temple its common name. You can get your fortune told here. ⓐ Race Course Rd ⓛ 07.00–18.00 ⓝ MRT: Little India. Small donation for fortune telling

Sri Srinivasa Perumal Temple

This temple comes into its own at Thaipusam (see pages 14–15) when the devotees and their families gather to prepare themselves for the big march to Tank Road. Perumal, the incarnation of Vishnu to whom the temple is dedicated, is the god of mercy and preserver of the universe. A temple to Perumal was first built here in 1885 but the modern building dates back to the 1960s. The five-tiered *gopuram* (entry gate) covered in images of Vishnu in his various incarnations was constructed in 1975. ⓐ 397 Serangoon Rd ⓛ 06.00–12.00, 17.00–21.00 ⓝ MRT: Farrer Park

Sri Veeramakaliamman Temple

Dedicated to the Hindu goddess Kali – a complex mixture of annihilation and benevolence and the wife of the god Shiva – this is one of the most popular temples in Singapore. It was

THE CITY

originally built in the late 19th century by South Indian labourers who had settled around Buffalo Road, then added to over the years. The enormous Disney-like *gopuram* was constructed in 1987. Visitors to the temple are welcome but should be considerately dressed and remove their shoes. Inside, the various incarnations of the goddess are represented; one shows a necklace of the skulls of her victims, while others show her in more peaceful modes. Also represented here are Kali's sons Murugan and Ganesh, the elephant-headed god. There is always a buzz of activity in the

🔺 *Singapore's biggest mosque: Sultan Mosque*

DEEPAVALI

The Indian festival of lights sees the area around Serangoon Road come even more alive. The month-long festival, which celebrates an ancient victory of the Hindu god Lord Krishna over a demon called Narakasura, fills the road with decorations and lights. Bazaars selling Indian delicacies and goods spring up in the side streets, and homes are lit with tiny oil lamps as an offering to Lakshmi who will bring prosperity to any house she visits. On the day of the festival Hindus carefully prepare themselves with oil, put on fresh clothes and attend the temple. The festival occurs some time between October and November.

temple, with worshippers bringing coconuts and bananas to offer the goddess and dhoti-wearing priests attending to them. Often there are wonderful performances of clashing instruments and other events. ⓐ 141 Serangoon Rd ⓑ 08.00–12.30, 16.00–20.30 ⓝ MRT: Little India

Sultan Mosque

Singapore's biggest and most central mosque was built in 1925 to a design by English architects Swan and Maclaren. Take away the dome and minarets and there's a distinctly British municipal feel to the place. Visitors can only go into the entrance lobby and must remove shoes and keep shoulders and legs covered. Avoid Fridays when the mosque is very busy. ⓐ Bussorah St ⓑ 09.00–13.00 ⓝ MRT: Bugis; Bus: 7, 32, 51, 63, 80, 145, 197

THE CITY

RETAIL THERAPY

Bugis Junction Upmarket shopping centre, incorporating some old streets that are now glass-covered and entirely air-conditioned, with a Japanese department store and more retail outlets than you will have time to visit. Check out the beauty treatments at Missha (02-22) and The Face Shop next door. ⓐ 200 Victoria St ⓘ 6557 6557 ⓒ 10.30–21.30 Ⓜ MRT: Bugis

Jamal Kazura Aromatics Specialist shop selling oils for perfumes and aromatherapy. You can buy the oils in different amounts, from 10 ml to 250 ml, with storage bottles also for sale. ⓐ 137 Dunlop St ⓘ 6392 1978 ⓒ 10.00–20.30 Tues–Sun, 12.00–20.30 Mon Ⓜ MRT: Little India

Jyothi Fabrics Silk and lace, mostly from Korea, sold by the metre and varying in price from S$10 to S$300 per metre. There is another outlet, Manisha: The Fabric Palace, also in Arab Street (no. 67). ⓐ 63 Arab St ⓘ 6296 4784 ⓒ 11.00–18.30 Ⓜ MRT: Bugis

MKM Bangles, chokers, gold nosestuds, anklets and costume jewellery – all in a glorious array of colours. ⓐ 90 Serangoon Rd ⓘ 6294 2903 ⓒ 10.00–20.30 Ⓜ MRT: Little India

Mustafa Centre An excellent department store, unbeatable for luggage (second floor), which also has a supermarket and pharmacy. This shop is almost a sight in itself, filled with people loading up with suitcases and electrical goods at two in the morning.

(a) 145 Syed Alwi Rd (t) 6295 5855 (w) www.mustafa.com.sg
(c) 24 hrs (m) MRT: Farrer Park (Exit A)

Saadullah Carpets from Iran, India and Pakistan. Some are small enough to carry home with you but overseas delivery is also an option. (a) 45 Arab St (t) 6296 8545 (w) www.tawakacarpets.com
(c) 10.00–20.00 (m) MRT: Bugis

San Marco Collection An attractive shop retailing its own designs in home-made jewellery and precious stones and, as well, a nice line in ethnic clothing from India and Nepal. Come here for that belly dancing outfit you have been looking for. (a) 29 Arab St
(t) 6293 3379 (c) 10.00–19.30 Mon–Sat, 12.00–18.00 Sun (m) MRT: Bugis

Sim Lim Square The place to go for electronics and anything else gadgety. Avoid the shops on the first floor, plunge into the depths of the mall, and prepare to haggle. (a) 1 Rochor Canal Rd
(c) 11.00–22.00 (m) MRT: Bugis

Sultan Ahmet Lamps, water pipes, cushion and bed covers, ceramics – the merchandise all comes from Turkey. (a) 31 Arab St
(t) 6294 6070 (c) 10.00–21.00 (m) MRT: Bugis

Tabletop Creations Facing Sultan Mosque, this store has a good selection of items such as batik fans, bags, scarves and shawls, sets of fancy chopsticks, hand woven baskets and the usual range of T-shirts. Good for small gifts and souvenirs. (a) 46 Bussorah St
(t) 6341 7381 (c) 09.00–18.00 Mon–Sat, 09.00–17.00 Sun (m) MRT: Bugis

THE CITY

TAKING A BREAK

Ananda Bhavan £ ❶ First-class vegetarian Indian eatery and, if you order the *paper masala thosai*, you won't get a longer (length, not time) meal anywhere in Singapore. The daily specials are always interesting. Walking from the MRT station towards Serangoon Road, you pass Ananda Bhavan on your right. There is also a branch at 58 Serangoon Road, opposite the Mustafa Centre. ⓐ Blk 663, 01-10 Buffalo Rd ❶ 6297 9522 ⓦ www.anandabhavan.com ⓛ 08.00–20.30 Ⓝ MRT: Little India

Chola's £ ❷ This is convenient for a quick bite in between shopping at the Mustafa Centre, which is just at the top of the road. Mostly meat dishes but also two vegetarian set meals. Chicken and *biriyanis*, and lots of *dosai*, *utthappam*, *sooji* and *idlies*. ⓐ 115 Syed Alwi Rd St ❶ 6396 8859 ⓛ 06.00–00.00 Ⓝ MRT: Farrer Park

Kampong Glam Café £ ❸ A pleasant place for an iced drink or a traditional Malay dish like *tahu goreng*, *roti kirai* or *gado-gado*. Tables outside on the pavement. ⓐ 17 Bussorah St ❶ 6294 8923 ⓛ 08.00–00.00 Ⓝ MRT: Bugis

Mubarak Restaurant £ ❹ Recommended for a *roti prata* breakfast or mid-morning break, before or after a spot of shopping on Serangoon Road. Tables on the pavement, on the corner of Campbell Lane and Clive Street. ⓐ 21 Campbell Lane ❶ 6337 1464 ⓛ 06.00–00.00 Ⓝ MRT: Little India

LITTLE INDIA & ARAB STREET

AFTER DARK

RESTAURANTS

Blue Jaz £ ❺ Local and Western food plus various smoothies and beers help make this small joint a suitable venue for relaxing at a pavement table after the sun, and the traffic, has gone down. ⓐ 11 Bali Lane, off North Bridge Rd ⓣ 6297 1280 ⓛ 10.30–22.30 ⓜ MRT: Bugis

Madras New Woodlands Restaurant £ ❻ No self-respecting tourist should leave Singapore without visiting the city state's most famous vegetarian restaurant. It offers an amazing range of breads served in little steel trays with pots of tongue-lashing curries and cooling *laksis*. Great. ⓐ 12–14 Upper Dickson Rd ⓣ 6293 6980 ⓛ 07.00–22.30 ⓜ MRT: Little India

Mustard £ ❼ A good alternative if you don't fancy the fish-head curry joints on this road. The terrific Northern Indian cuisine here makes a nice change from the usual naan bread/chicken tikka masala combo. Popular in the evenings with locals and tourists. ⓐ 32 Race Course Rd ⓣ 6297 8422 ⓛ 11.30–15.00, 18.00–22.45 Mon–Fri, 11.30–22.45 Sat & Sun ⓜ MRT: Little India

Zam Zam Restaurant £ ❽ This wonderful old Muslim restaurant on North Bridge Road celebrated its centenary in 2008 and, one is inclined to think, the *murtabaks* taste as good as ever. Good value meals and tables upstairs with plenty of room. ⓐ 697 North Bridge Rd ⓣ 6298 7011 ⓛ 08.00–23.00 ⓜ MRT: Bugis

THE CITY

Alaturka ££ ❾ Turkish and Mediterranean food in a neat little restaurant that makes an effort to evoke a non-Asian atmosphere. Mezzes, kebabs, pide, pizzas and seafood. ⓐ 16 Bussorah St ❶ 6294 0304 ⓦ www.alaturka.com.sg ⓛ 11.00–23.00 ⓝ MRT: Bugis

Banana Leaf Apolo ££ ❿ Terrific Indian restaurant with a menu that has stood the test of time. The all-time favourite here is the fish head curry. This is the original branch, in existence since 1974, though there is now also a branch at 48 Serangoon Road.

▲ *Try the fish head curry at Banana Leaf Apolo – it's superb!*

LITTLE INDIA & ARAB STREET

54 Race Course Rd 6293 8682 www.bananaleafapolo.com
 10.30–22.30 MRT: Farrer Park

Olive Tree Restaurant ££ ⓫ Excellent all-day buffets with a gastronomic spread of meat and seafood, although the offerings on Friday and Saturday nights go over the top on seafood. A hearty Champagne brunch on Sunday. Hotel Inter-Continental, 80 Middle Rd 6825 1061 06.00–10.30, 12.00–14.30, 18.00–22.00 Mon–Fri; 06.00–10.30, 12.30–17.30, 19.00–22.30 Sat & Sun MRT: Bugis

BARS
Prince of Wales Prince of Wales Backpacker Hostel bar with live music Monday to Saturday kicking off at 21.30 and a live mic session on Sunday nights. Affordable beer. 101 Dunlop St 6299 0130 www.pow.com.sg MRT: Bugis, Little India

CHIJMES ££ ⓬
Chijmes is a one-stop, evening food-and-drink venue where there is a good choice of restaurants and themed pubs, plus an open area with a large screen showing international sports fixtures. The best restaurant for Mediterranean-style food is the candlelit **Esmirada**; you should not be disappointed by the skewered meat, seafood paella or the mussels. 30 Victoria St 6336 3684 www.esmirada.com 18.00–22.30 Sun–Thur, 18.00–23.00 Fri & Sat MRT: City Hall

THE CITY

Boat Quay & Chinatown

Once the commercial hub of the city, this area has long since abandoned its bumboats and *coolie wallahs* for designer restaurants and cool bars. Its huge, once-crumbling warehouses now provide a playground for the young and restless, and the elderly public buildings of the British Empire have been given a shiny makeover and turned over to the tourist trade. Like Arab Street and Serangoon Road, the whole lifestyle of the area has been packaged into easy-to-chew bites of colourful Chinese life. But sneak past the tourist itinerary and you'll find a little of the old ways – strange things in tubs waiting to become dinner, paper products to burn for the ancestors, weird and wonderful medicinal items, fire walking in the temples, and shops where some serious bargaining, Chinese style, is *de rigueur*.

● *The Boat Quay area is very colourful*

BOAT QUAY & CHINATOWN

SIGHTS & ATTRACTIONS

Amoy Street

Once densely populated by people from the Xiamen province of China, the street has mostly undergone some serious gentrification. Where once tiny shops spilled their wares out onto the five foot ways (see page 49), now trendy businesses have renovated the old shophouses. Some of them have been beautifully done, and you can see the bat-shaped ventilation grills, red doors and symbols warding off the bad *chi* that travels in straight lines along the streets. On the corner of Amoy Street (*no. 66*) is a still active place of worship, the Sin Chor Kung Temple, painted bright red to draw in some good luck, and guarded by two stone lions and some huge pots of ash from burned incense sticks.
Ⓜ MRT: Raffles Place, Chinatown

Far East Square

Entirely constructed as part of the renovation of Chinatown, this area, with the Fuk Tak Chi Temple at its heart, has become a major lunch stop for busy office workers. The food halls bear little resemblance, either in atmosphere or cost, to the hawker centres of old but they are air-conditioned and very popular.
Ⓜ MRT: Raffles Place

Sago Street

This street was once the very heart of Chinatown. It was home for decades to death houses, places where the very elderly were taken to die, and contained both the death houses themselves and several coffin makers. It was part of Chinese belief that having

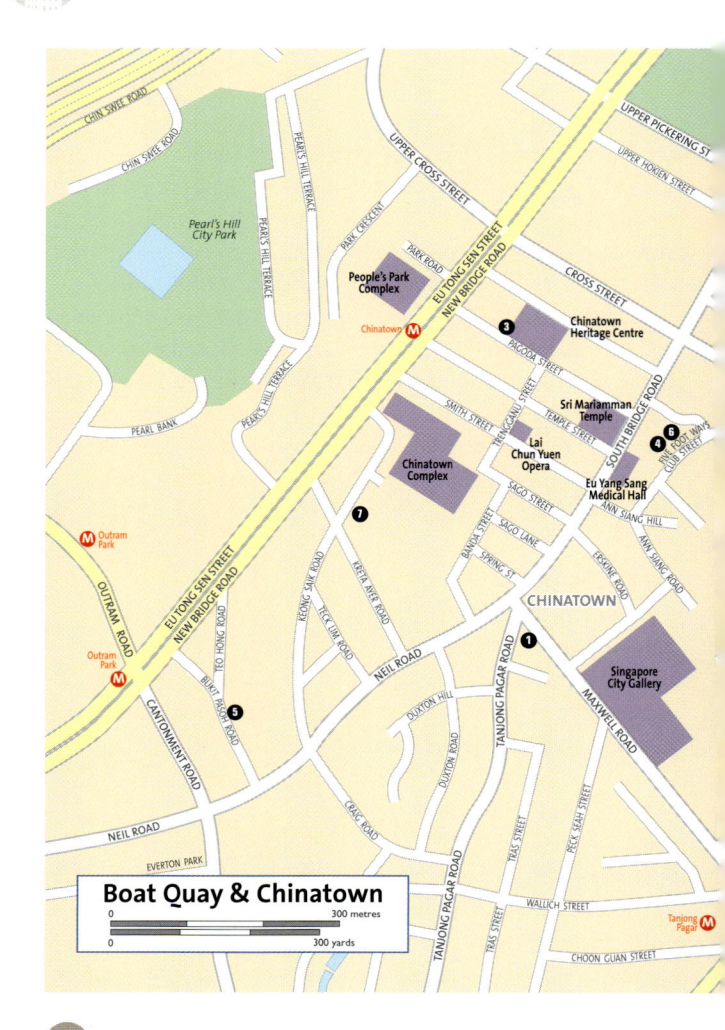

THE CITY

Boat Quay & Chinatown

BOAT QUAY & CHINATOWN

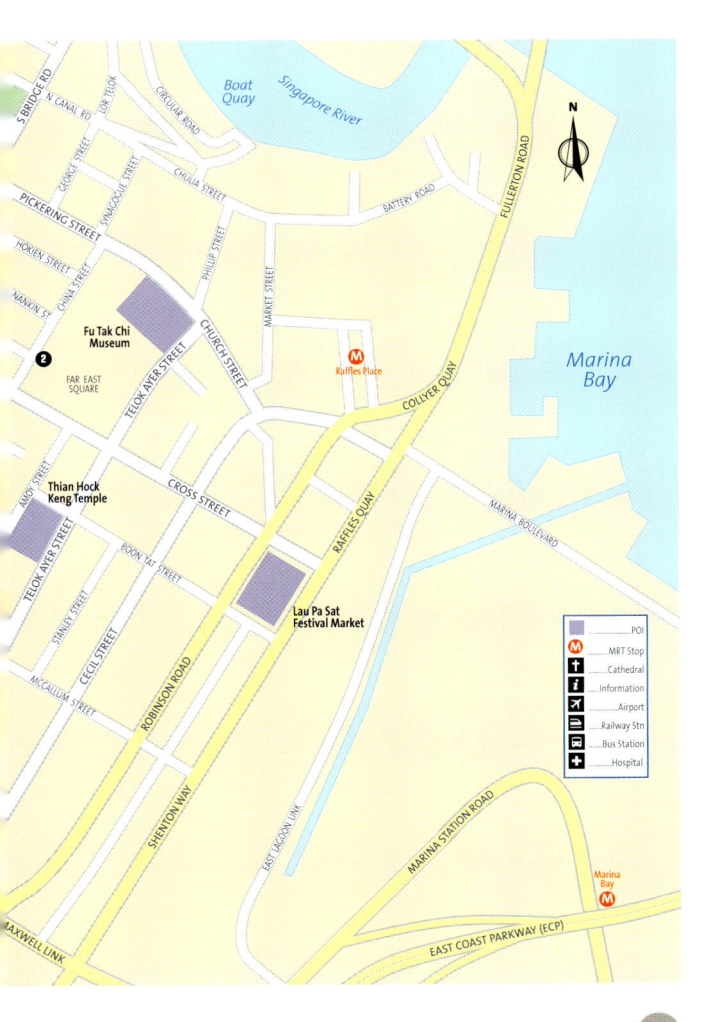

THE CITY

someone die in the home was bad luck so the elderly, one assumes, cheerfully went off to these places. Now gentrified, the street comes alive during Chinese New Year when it is filled with stalls and decorations. Perhaps as a memory to the thousands of elderly people who came here to die, a little concrete seating area, Trishaw Park, provides a quiet spot to meet and chat. Seriously dedicated visitors can hire a rickshaw here for a trip around the area. As it morphs into Trengganu Street, you will see that some of the old businesses struggle on. Trengganu Street was once a red light area, home to Japanese prostitutes. At the corner with Smith Street is Lai Chun Yuen, a former Cantonese opera house which still retains much of its original architecture. On the opposite corner is the Chinatown Complex market and food centre, where you can stroll around the wetmarket and be

⬤ *Junction of Smith and Trengganu streets*

amazed at what the locals are buying for dinner. Here you may well catch sight of a bill being tallied with an abacus. In some of the backstreets around here (Smith Street, Kreta Ayer Road, Keong Saik Road) you will see what at first seems completely mad – household goods made entirely of bamboo sticks covered in tissue paper and painted. These are still very popular gifts for the departed. The paper goods are burned and their essence floats up in the smoke to provide for the ancestors. Around Sago Street you will see Mercedes cars, laptops, Philippina maids, washing machines, men's suits, three-piece suites, credit cards – if it exists on Earth and brings its owner status, then you can buy it here.
Ⓝ MRT: Chinatown

South Bridge Road

This very busy main street is the economic heart of Chinatown. Like the rest of Chinatown its traditional small shops are giving way to renovated tourist-orientated boutiques selling antiques and designer nicknacks for the modern home. A few of the older residents hang in there, and the street is home to the Sri Mariamman Hindu Temple and the Eu Yan Sang Medical Hall, both places that have resisted the tidying up of the area.
Ⓝ MRT: Chinatown, Bus: 51, 63, 80, 124, 145, 166, 174, 174e, 197

CULTURE

Chinatown Heritage Centre

If you visit only one of Singapore's museums you should make it this one. The 200 or so years of Chinese immigration into Singapore has been collected into this fascinating museum, made up of three renovated shophouses. A journey through the museum, accompanied by a soundtrack of period music and the noise of the shophouses, starts off with a model of one of the junks that the immigrant workers arrived in and goes on to tell of their safe landing and settlement in this area. Using personal accounts by Chinese residents whose memories go back to the early years of the last century, the museum recreates much of what has been lost in the gentrification of the area – the history of the clan associations, the wars between rival secret societies, the work in the quays and other places. Whole rooms are recreated, including one of the Sago Street death houses, and the terrible living conditions of the workers are brought home. On a lighter note there are original hawker stalls, a coffee shop and lots of things familiar to older visitors – toys made in Singapore, adverts for commodities from the 1950s and much more. ❸ 48 Pagoda St ❶ 6325 2878 ❿ www.chinatownheritage.com.sg ❻ 09.00–20.00 Ⓜ MRT: Chinatown. Admission charge (free guided tours)

Eu Yan Sang Medical Hall
Dispensers of traditional Chinese medicine, medical halls were once the main form of medical treatment available to the poor of Singapore. Eu Yan Sang started off his business in Perak in 1879, and expanded first to Singapore in 1910 then as far as Hong Kong and China. Part tourist attraction and part medicine shop, the three renovated art deco shophouses are filled with all sorts of dried and preserved things you really wouldn't want to eat but which, apparently, are very good for you – lizards, scorpions, snakes, all manner of dried fungus, internal (and external!) organs of assorted creatures and, of course, ginseng, which is doled out

SRI MARIAMMAN TEMPLE

This is Singapore's oldest Hindu temple, built before the island was divided into ethnic quarters and founded by Naraina Pillay, an Indian official who arrived in Singapore aboard the same vessel as Raffles. The brick building was erected in 1843 and is dedicated to Mariamman, the goddess of healing. Other gods figure here, as they do in other Hindu temples. At the left of the entrance is Krishna and at the right is Rama, while the gold figure at the bottom of the frieze is Mariamman. Inside, the walls and ceiling are covered in pictures of assorted deities and there are shrines to Periachiamman, to whom small babies are brought for protection, and Sri Aravan. During the Thimithi Festival devotees to the goddess line up in their hundreds to run barefoot across hot coals inside the temple. If you are here during the festival be prepared for big crowds and a lot of yelling. 244 South Bridge Rd 6223 4064 06.00–12.30, 16.00–21.30 MRT: Chinatown; Bus: 2, 12, 33, 51, 61, 62, 63, 81, 84, 103, 124, 143, 145, 147, 166, 174, 190, 197, 851. Charge for camera usage

to visitors in the form of tea. Whatever your complaint there is a cure and since the place has been operating for more than 100 years you can probably trust that the cure won't do you any harm. Probably. 267–71 South Bridge Rd 6223 6333 www.euyansang.com 08.30–18.00 Mon–Sat MRT: Chinatown

THE CITY

Fu Tak Chi Museum

Beautifully renovated, this former temple was established by the Hakka community in the early 19th century and functioned well into the late 20th century. It is a lovely building, its decorated roof and interior door gods well preserved, but is now a museum to the old ways of Chinatown. Displays include a diorama of what this area once looked like, opium-smoking paraphernalia, old clothes and a model of a junk. It's not up to the standard of the Chinatown Heritage Centre, but as a well lit example of a temple building it's certainly worth a visit. ⓐ Telok Ayer St ⓛ 10.00–22.00 Mon–Thur, 09.00–21.00 Fri–Sun Ⓜ MRT: Raffles Place

Singapore City Gallery

This government-owned exhibition space might seem a little dull at first glance but is actually quite fascinating. It contains an exhibition of Singapore's plans for urban renewal, and considering the determination, cash and engineering that gets put into Singapore's schemes it is well worth a visit to be amazed. The exhibition demonstrates just how much of what you take for granted as Singapore was once the open sea. New land reclamation projects, urban renewal schemes and plans for renovating places of historical significance are all laid out in a series of interactive displays. You can also plan your own little bit of the city and play around with the webcam above the building. You'll find yourself torn between admiration for the scope of it all and despair at just how controlled and regulated this tiny city state is. ⓐ 45 Maxwell Rd ⓣ 6321 8321 ⓦ www.ura.gov.sg ⓛ 09.00–17.00 Mon–Sat Ⓜ MRT: Chinatown

Thian Hock Keng Temple

This temple in Telok Ayer Street is the oldest Taoist temple in Singapore and is dedicated to Tin Hou, the goddess who protects seafarers. Its name translates into the Temple of Heavenly Happiness. When it was built it occupied a prime site on the waterfront and would have been the first place that Hokkien travellers came to thank the deities for their safe arrival. The current building was begun in 1839 when the statue of the goddess was brought in from southern China. The elaborate roof tiles are delft and the supporting pillars, like the goddess, come from southern China. The railings are from Glasgow. Stone lions guard the doors and all manner of wildlife is incorporated into the roof. Next door to the temple is a tiny patch of green called Telok Sayer Green and next door again is the Nagore Durgha shrine, built by southern Indian Chulias. ⓐ 158 Telok Ayer St ⓘ 6423 4616 ⓒ 08.30–21.00 ⓜ MRT: Raffles Place ; Bus: 2, 12, 33, 51, 61, 62, 63, 81, 84, 103, 124, 143, 145, 147, 166, 174, 190, 197, 851

RETAIL THERAPY

Pagoda Street Good for souvenirs, gifts, T-shirts and the like. Some schlock but also places like Scarlet Thread (no. 57), a superior art and craft shop. ⓐ Pagoda St ⓒ 10.00–23.00 ⓜ MRT: Chinatown

People's Park Complex This is what shopping in Singapore used to be like before cookie-cutter air-conditioned malls took over. One floor is dedicated to fabric stalls with the widest range of silks, linens and designer materials you'll probably ever find. ⓐ 1 Park Rd ⓒ 11.00–20.00 ⓜ MRT: Chinatown

THE CITY

Sago Street Best to stroll down here at night when the street is pedestrianised and the stalls are out on the pavement. Come here for Chinese slippers, jade wristbands, jewellery and silk garments that will make you look like a Singapore Airlines hostess. Nothing here is expensive, and prices are mostly marked and more-or-less fixed. 🕒 10.00–23.00 Ⓝ MRT: Chinatown

TAKING A BREAK

Maxwell Food Centre £ ❶ One of the few unreconstructed food centres in central Singapore, complete with whirling fans. Some very slithery tastes from the Chinese outlets – a noticeboard outside explains some of the more exotic concoctions. Vegetarian food can be found at Mr Bean (no. 11), and at no. 37. There is also an Indian outlet serving *murtabaks* and *roti*. ⓐ Maxwell Rd 🕒 08.30–20.30 Ⓝ MRT: Chinatown or Outram Park

Ya Kun £ ❷ The original Ya Kun coffee shop in what is now a chain of similarly named premises. The menu here is identical, except for the prices, to the one that first greeted customers in 1944. Be sure to try the Ya Kun toast with an egg to dip it in. Tables indoors and out. ⓐ 01-01 Far East Square, 18 China St ⓘ 6438 3638 Ⓦ www.yakun.com 🕒 07.30–19.00 Mon–Fri, 08.00–18.00 Sat & Sun Ⓝ MRT: Chinatown

AFTER DARK

RESTAURANTS
Singapore Heritage Restaurant £ ❸ A bit kitschy but a likeable

BOAT QUAY & CHINATOWN

and inoffensive café that serves up old Chinese favourites like chilli crab sauce but adds spaghetti just for fun. The satay and mango chicken rice are well worth tasting. ⓐ 46 Pagoda St ⓣ 6225 2001 ⓛ 11.00–23.00 Ⓜ MRT: Chinatown

Jerry's ££ ❹ Jerry's is the place for ribs and steaks. Space is limited, so make a reservation, either indoors or outside on the five foot ways pavement under two slowly whirling fans. Cocktails and world beers available. ⓐ 92 Club St ⓣ 6323 4550 Ⓦ www.jerrybbq.com.sg ⓛ 12.00–22.00 Sun–Thurs, 12.00–22.30 Fri & Sat Ⓜ MRT: Chinatown

Majestic Restaurant ££ ❺ Serves cutting-edge Cantonese food, such as crispy wasabi prawns and Peking duck served with spiced foie gras. The décor is equally modern, with an open kitchen design and dining tables under ceiling portholes that look up into the hotel's swimming pool. ⓐ New Majestic Hotel, 31 Bukit Pasoh Rd ⓣ 6511 4700 ⓛ 12.00–14.30, 18.30–22.00 Ⓜ MRT: Outram Park

Senso ££ ❻ Italian fine dining in an alfresco courtyard setting or indoors in air-conditioned comfort. Either way you will enjoy well-prepared Italian dishes like fettuccine with lobster in a fragrant herb sauce. A modernist bar serves cocktails and aperitifs. ⓐ 21 Club St ⓣ 6224 3534 ⓛ 12.00–14.30, 18.00–22.30 Mon–Fri, 18.00–22.30 Sat & Sun Ⓜ MRT: Chinatown

Ember Restaurant ££–£££ ❼ Advance booking is fairly essential at this popular European restaurant where the food, décor and style of service is all very contemporary. ⓐ Hotel 1929, 50 Keong Saik Rd ⓣ 6347 1928 ⓛ 11.30–14.00, 18.30–22.00 Ⓜ MRT: Chinatown

THE CITY

BARS & CLUBS

DYMK It's hard to miss this bar, with its red-and-yellow exterior screaming out for attention amongst a row of more modest joints. But the vibe inside is all chilled – if you think it's too early (or late) for a cocktail, have a coffee and a slice of cake instead. Retro hits on the second floor. ⓐ 9 Kreta Ayer Rd ⓣ 6224 3965 ⓦ www.dymk.sg ⓛ 19.00–00.00 Tues–Thur, 19.00–01.00 Fri, 20.00–02.00 Sat ⓜ MRT: Chinatown

Home If you're bored with try-hard, overpriced mainstream monstrosities, you belong here. Home supports local bands and DJs, and plays an eclectic mix of punk, techno, indie and deep house. The sofas are incredibly comfy – if you're lucky enough to find an empty seat. ⓐ B1-01/06 The Riverwalk, 20 Upper Circular Rd ⓣ 9877 6055 ⓦ www.homeclub.com.sg ⓛ 21.00–03.00 Tues–Thur, 22.00–06.00 Fri & Sat ⓜ MRT: Clarke Quay

Zouk Well-established nightclub that now comprises three venues – Phuture, Velvet Underground and Zouk itself – and continues to attract a hip crowd. There is a happy hour on Friday & Saturday between 23.00 and 00.00. ⓐ 17 Jiak Kim St, off Kim Seng Rd ⓣ 6738 2988 ⓦ www.zoukclub.com.sg ⓛ 21.00–04.00 Wed, Fri & Sat ⓜ MRT: Clarke Quay; Bus: 54 (from Scotts Rd), 32, 195 (from City Hall MRT station)

▶ *A quiet beach on the island of Sentosa*

OUT OF TOWN trips

OUT OF TOWN

Sentosa & Western Singapore

To the west of the island, beyond the waves of high-rise public housing and modern town centres, there are several places to visit. The Singapore Science Centre will keep children busy for hours, while the Jurong Bird Park is a genuinely fascinating place. Haw Par Villa, renovated, failed and renovated again, is a shadow of its former self but worth the trip for the grisly scenes of damnation portrayed in its concrete statues. Sentosa defies description and just has to be visited. A law should be passed that no one can leave Singapore until they've spent a day there. Closer to home Holland Village is a shopper's dream, while the Botanic Gardens, near Orchard Road, makes a pleasant day out.

▲ *Cacti in the Cactus Garden at the Botanic Gardens*

SENTOSA & WESTERN SINGAPORE

> **FAST-TRACK TRAVEL**
> Partially opened in 2007, but not due to be completed until 2010 or 2011, is a monorail system which is the fastest way to get to locations on Sentosa. Trains leave from the third level of VivoCity mall and run from 07.00–00.00. Tickets are S$3, which includes entry to Sentosa.

SIGHTS & ATTRACTIONS

Botanic Gardens

Carefully manicured, sporting all manner of weird and wonderful plants (make sure you spot the cannon ball trees!), the Botanic Gardens is a great place to visit. Come early in the morning to watch the tai chi exercises; come at dusk to venture into the tiny patch of virgin rainforest and imagine you're in the jungle; or just turn up in the middle of the day and wander. Best of all is the orchid garden filled with the most exotic orchids, many of them bred here and sporting names dumped on them to honour visiting foreign dignitaries. Afterwards pop into the hawker centre just by the main gate to savour what is possibly the best *roti john* and *tahu goreng* in town. ⓐ Holland Rd 🕒 05.00–00.00; National Orchid Garden: 08.30–19.00 🚌 Bus: 7, 75, 77, 105, 106, 123, 174. Admission charge for orchid garden

HarbourFront & Mount Faber

The best way to visit Sentosa, be scared witless and see some brilliant views at the same time is to arrive by cable-car from

OUT OF TOWN

MALAYSIA
Singapore
Borneo
Sumatra
Pulau Seletar
Selat Johor
Pasir Gudang
Yishun
Sungai Seletar Reservoir
Pulau Ubin
Jalan Kayu
Punggol
Changi Golf Club
Ferry to Desaru
Escape Theme Park
Seletar
Ang Mo Kio
Hougang
Changi
Singapore Changi Airport
Johore Battery
Changi Ferry Terminal
Phor Kark See Temple
Bedok Reservoir
Tampines
Changi Chapel & Museum
Paya Lebar
Sun Yat Sen Villa
Bedok
Geylang
Siglap
Kallang
Katong
Tanah Merah Ferry Terminal
Singapore National and Indoor Stadiums
SINGAPORE
Ferry to Bintan Island
Strait of Singapore
City
Large Town
Small Town
POI
Motorway
Main Road
Minor Road
Airport
Railway

OUT OF TOWN

Mount Faber. This has the added advantage of a visit to Mount Faber, which is worth the effort for the pretty park at the top of the hill. The easiest route to Mount Faber is via the cable-car from the HarbourFront, a huge new development of shops, marine terminals and restaurants – claimed to be the largest single shopping centre in Singapore, although how long that will last is anybody's guess. ⓝ Bus: 30, 65, 80, 97, 100, 145, 166, 855 to Telok Blangah Rd; Cable-car to Mount Faber from HarbourFront Tower 2: 08.30–23.00

Holland Village

Once the shopping centre for British troops stationed in army housing estates all around, Holland Village still retains a much more *gweilo*-orientated tone than some of the other suburbs of the city. The place is awash with craft, furniture and antique shops, as well as some good discount electrical stores. An afternoon shopping here, taking in lunch at one of the cafés or in the wetmarket, can be followed by an evening's entertainment in one of the several bars. ⓝ MRT: Buona Vista; Bus: 7, 61, 75, 77, 105, 106, 165, 970, 200

Jurong Bird Park

Hundreds of species of birds, many of them roaming free, live in this huge park. A whole day can be spent here, visiting the various houses, the walk-through aviary and the bird shows. When you arrive be sure to note down the times of the shows and get to them – they are fascinating and because of the size of the place they are easy to miss. ⓐ 2 Jurong Hill ⓣ 6265 0022 ⓦ www.birdpark.com.sg ⓛ 08.30–18.00 ⓝ MRT: Boon Lay; Bus: 194, 251. Admission charge

Sentosa

It may not be an earthly paradise, but it couldn't be anywhere else than Singapore. This place is how Singaporeans like their fun – organised, noisy, crowded and in the worst possible taste. If your idea of a good time is a night at the theatre followed by supper and a quiet glass of wine, don't come here. If you like history, fun fairs, water rides, tacky souvenir shops and dancing fountains, this place is essential. Underwater World is a truly fascinating experience. Strangely there are also areas of undisturbed wildlife, empty beaches and some very classy hotels. ⓝ Sentosa bus from HarbourFront 07.00–23.00 Sun–Thur, 07.00–00.30 Fri & Sat; SIA hop-on hop-off bus from Clarke Quay 10.00–18.00; cable-car from Mount Faber and HarbourFront Tower 2: 08.30–23.00. Admission charge to island and to each sight

🔺 *Loris feeding at Jurong Bird Park*

OUT OF TOWN

CULTURE

Fort Siloso
Here you'll find a series of coastal fortifications built by the British and occupied by them from the 1880s until they were surrendered to the Japanese in 1942, when Sentosa became a prisoner of war camp and base for the Japanese. The story of the fort is presented in an entertaining way; what's more, there are tunnels to wander, big guns and some great views.
ⓐ 33 Allanbrooke Rd, Sentosa ⓣ 6276 0388 ⓦ www.sentosa.com.sg
ⓛ 10.00–18.00 ⓝ Bus to Sentosa/cable-car, then Blue or Red bus line, then Fort Train. Admission charge

Haw Par Villa
Built by the brothers who marketed Tiger Balm oil, this is a theme park with a difference. Hundreds of concrete statues portray the horrors that will befall sinners in the many layers of hell. Just to cheer you up are more statues of good things happening in heaven plus some weird and wonderful creatures, but it's the torture images that will stay with you. Kids love it. ⓐ 262 Pasir Panjang Rd ⓣ 6872 2780 ⓛ 09.00–19.00 ⓝ MRT: Buona Vista, then bus 200

Images of Singapore Exhibition
An interactive history of Singapore with wax figures in traditional costumes, leading figures in the island's history dioramas, all culminating in the Surrender Chambers where the history of World War II and the final surrender of the Japanese is

recounted. This is Singapore as it wants to be seen. Fascinating. ⓐ 33 Allanbrooke Road, Sentosa ⓣ 1800 736 8672 ⓦ www.sentosa.com.sg ⓛ 09.00–19.00 ⓝ Bus to Sentosa/cable-car, then Blue or Red bus line, then Fort Train. Admission charge

Singapore Science Centre
Like all good science centres, this one has knobs to pull, screens to press, huge pieces of noisy moving equipment and hours of fascinating engagement with the physical world. It also has plagues of schoolchildren, just like all the other science centres you've ever been to. Good fun, but avoid school hours. The Omnimax Theatre shows scary movies on an enormous screen. ⓐ 15 Science Centre Rd ⓣ 6425 2500 ⓦ www.science.edu.sg ⓛ Science Centre: 10.00–18.00 Tues–Sun; Omnimax: 10.00–20.00 Tues–Sun ⓝ MRT: Jurong East; Bus: 66, 178, 198, 335. Admission charge for Science Centre and Omnimax

Tiger Brewery
The brewery making the famous beer of Singapore, which perfumes the air of Jurong and cools the palate in so many hawker centres, is open to the public for guided tours. Be prepared for a movie about the company and its history, a tour through the shiny high-tech works and several hours in the bar checking that the brew is just right. ⓐ 459 Jalan Ahmad Ibrahim ⓣ 6860 3007 ⓦ www.apb.com.sg ⓛ Tours (which must be booked in advance): 10.30, 14.00, 16.00, 18.30 Mon–Fri ⓝ MRT: Boon Lay, then bus 182. Admission charge

OUT OF TOWN

RETAIL THERAPY

Lim's Art & Living Singapore has a reputation for excellent arts and crafts. Lim's has an illustrious history, dating back to the 1960s when it started selling Asian artefacts to British troops, and is still one of the best places for decorative items for the home. ⓐ 02-01 Holland Rd Shopping Centre, 211 Holland Ave ⓣ 6467 1300 ⓒ 10.00–20.30 Ⓝ MRT: Buona Vista

Vista & Co Following in the footsteps of Lim's Art & Living, this is another shop in the Holland Village neighbourhood with attractive Asian-style items such as Chinese opera masks, mahjong sets, bead curtains and porcelain lamp stands. ⓐ 02-30 Holland Rd Shopping Centre, 211 Holland Ave ⓣ 6466 6276 ⓒ 10.00–20.30 Ⓝ MRT: Buona Vista

VivoCity Singapore's latest retail destination, convenient to visit when travelling to or from Sentosa; it has more than 300 outlets devoted to shopping, eating and drinking, and entertainment. Marks & Spencer and Tangs are two of the big-name tenants; there is also a multiplex cinema and an outdoor amphitheatre on the third level with fine views of the offshore scene. ⓐ HarbourFront ⓣ 6469 5647 ⓒ 10.00–20.30 Ⓝ MRT: HarbourFront

TAKING A BREAK

Crystal Jade Kitchen £ A suitable venue for a speedy Chinese lunch, with a choice of delicious *dim sum*, fried spring rolls,

noodles and *congee*. 🅐 2 Lorong Mambong, Holland Village
🅣 6475 8174 🕐 09.30–21.00 Ⓝ MRT: Buona Vista

New Zealand Natural £ For delicious ice creams made of 100 per cent natural ingredients, plus smoothies, fruit juices and waffles, visit Sentosa's branch of the trendy international chain of ice cream parlours. 🅐 50 Siloso Walk Beach, Sentosa
🅣 6273 1971 🅦 www.nzn.com.sg 🕐 11.00–22.00 Ⓝ Bus to Sentosa/cable-car, then Blue, Red bus line or Siloso Beach tram

San Katong Laksa £ An informal setting for the enjoyment of *laksa*, a filling noodle soup with dried shrimps, coconut milk, slices of fishcake and prawns. Good local coffee too.
🅐 29B Lorong Liput, Holland Village 🅣 6468 5415 🕐 09.30–22.00
Ⓝ MRT: Buona Vista

Thai Express £ Tasty bites like Thai fried squid, *popiah* wraps and clever concoctions with tofu help give plenty of choice to all comers. 🅐 16 Lorong Mambong, Holland Village 🅣 6466 6766
🕐 11.30–22.30 Mon–Thur, 11.30–23.30 Fri & Sat, 11.30–23.00 Sun
Ⓝ MRT: Buona Vista

AFTER DARK

RESTAURANTS
Baden Restaurant and Pub ££ A long-established German-style restaurant where, once you step into the dark teakwood interior, the Orient feels like a continent away. Tuck into steak or pork knuckles washed down with jugs of Bavarian beer. 🅐 42 Lorong

OUT OF TOWN

Mambong, Holland Village ☎ 6475 1270 ⏰ 18.30–22.30 Ⓝ MRT: Buona Vista

Michelangelo's ££ Upmarket Italian restaurant patronised by the local expat community who come here for the vodka penne before a main course and a tiramisu and brownies afterwards. 📍 01-60 Block 44 Chip Bee Gardens, Jalan Merah Saga, Holland Village ☎ 6475 9069 🌐 www.michelangelos.com.sg ⏰ 11.30–14.30, 18.30–23.00 Sun–Fri, 18.30–23.00 Sat Ⓝ MRT: Buona Vista

Original Sin ££ A vegetarian and vegan restaurant, with signature dishes of risotto, *bosco misto* (tofu patties) and a mezze platter. 📍 01-62 Block 43 Chip Bee Gardens, Jalan Merah Saga, Holland Village ☎ 6475 5605 🌐 www.originalsin.com.sg ⏰ 11.30–14.30, 18.30–23.00 Tues–Sun Ⓝ MRT: Buona Vista

Min Jiang ££–£££ The large-sized bungalows of Rochester Park were once home to British officers – the lower ranks were crowded into Chip Bee Gardens – and have now been converted into classy restaurants. Min Jiang's speciality is Beijing Duck prepared in a wood-fired oven. 📍 5 Rochester Park, Rochester Park ☎ 6774 0122 ⏰ 11.00–14.30, 18.00–22.30 Ⓝ MRT: Buona Vista

Sky Dining £££ For a meal with a difference, splash out on a three-course meal in a cable-car, while it glides 70 m (230 ft) above the sea between Mount Faber and Sentosa. Western and continental set meals. The journey starts from The Jewel Box on Mount Faber. Advance reservation essential. Children's menu available. 📍 The Jewel Box, 109 Mount Faber Rd ☎ 6377 9688

SENTOSA & WESTERN SINGAPORE

🌐 www.mountfaber.com.sg/main-skydining.htm 🕐 18.30–20.30 🚇 Cable-car from HarbourFront Tower 2; Bus: Parks 409 (Sat, Sun & public holidays)

CLUBS

Wala Wala Café Bar One of the most popular nightspots in Holland Village, with an outdoor scene on the first level and live music up above. 📍 31 Lorong Mambong, Holland Village 📞 6462 4288 🕐 18.30–23.00 🚇 MRT: Buona Vista

ACCOMMODATION

Costa Sands Resort ££ If you fancy a night in Sentosa at reasonable prices try this place – huts and chalets, pool, café, barbecue pits and all the fun of Sentosa. 📍 30 Imbiah Walk, Sentosa 📞 6275 1034 🌐 www.costasands.com.sg 🚇 Bus to Sentosa/cable-car, then Siloso Beach tram

Rasa Sentosa Shangri La ££–£££ All the Shangri La luxury plus spa, beachfront accommodation, water sports, pool, whirlpool, gym, etc. 📍 101 Siloso Rd, Sentosa 📞 6275 0100 🌐 www.shangri-la.com 🚇 Bus to Sentosa/cable-car, then Blue, Red bus line or Siloso Beach tram

OUT OF TOWN

Bukit Timah, Changi & Bintan

In the northern and eastern areas of Singapore, all readily accessible by public transport in around 30 minutes, you'll find places to explore wildlife as well as some notable reminders of the island's role in World War II. The wildlife comes either neatly packaged at the zoo, or in its raw state at the Bukit Timah Nature Reserve or on Pulau Ubin, the perfect antidote to urban blues or consumer blow-out. Bukit Timah tends to be only mildly busy at weekends and public holidays; Singapore's zoo, with its enlightened approach to keeping and caging animals, is always full. Or, if you really want to get away from Singapore, why not visit Indonesia? From a ferry terminal at the eastern end of Singapore it is just a one-hour journey to the island of Bintan and, once there, you will really feel you are in Asia.

SIGHTS & ATTRACTIONS

Bintan

All you need is your passport and a US$10 note (for a visa) – obtainable from a money exchange at the ferry terminal – and you can be on Bintan in an hour. The island has a number of resort hotels, all owned and managed by Singaporean companies, where you can sunbathe under swaying palm trees, engage in water sports or indulge yourself at a luxury spa. The resort hotels all have their transport waiting at the arrival ferry terminal, and urban-weary travellers will soon find themselves in what the brochures call a 'sun-kissed paradise for fun-seekers'.

BUKIT TIMAH, CHANGI & BINTAN

Tanah Merah Ferry Terminal ⓣ 6542 4369 ⓦ www.brf.com.sg
ⓒ Ferries run from 09.10–20.00 Mon–Thur, 08.10–20.00 Fri–Sun

Bukit Timah Nature Reserve

The 164 m (538 ft) high Bukit Timah Hill, in central Singapore, is home to an area of primary rainforest within the city's limits – one of only two such places in the world (the other being Rio de Janeiro). What's more, it claims to have more plant species than the whole of North America. It certainly has macaques, snakes, giant ants, raucous bird life, monitor lizards, scorpions and pangolins, any of which you may encounter while wandering the well-signposted walkways. Go early in the morning when the wildlife is at its best, before the heat becomes oppressive

▲ *Escape to one of Bintan's lagoon resorts*

and the place fills up with joggers. ⓐ 177 Hindehede Dr
ⓘ 6468 5736 ⓦ www.nparks.gov.sg ⓒ Visitor centre:
08.30–18.00 ⓝ Bus: 67, 75, 170, 171, 173, 184, 852, 961

Joo Chiat Road, Changi
Beautifully restored Peranakan shophouses, especially those at
the junction of Koon Seng Road, with shops selling all manner
of things you'd like to take home. In the Joo Chiat Complex
there are glorious inexpensive silks, batik and carpets. ⓝ MRT:
Eunos; Bus: 15, 16, 33, 155

Kranji War Cemetery
The burial ground of Allied soldiers and the memorial that
commemorates the thousands who died are a moving sight.
Also here are the tombs of two former presidents of Singapore.
ⓐ 9 Woodlands Rd, Bukit Timah ⓒ 07.00–18.00 ⓝ MRT: Kranji;
Bus: 170

CHANGI MUSEUM
A harrowing account in the words, photographs and
artwork of some of those internees lucky enough to
have survived the Japanese occupation of the island.
Here also is a replica of the chapel built by inmates,
and lots of messages left by those who lost family
and friends here. ⓐ 1000 Upper Changi Rd ⓘ 6214 2451
ⓦ www.changimuseum.com ⓒ 09.30–17.00 ⓝ MRT:
Tanah Merah, then bus 2; Bus: 2, 29

Memories at Old Ford Factory

At the beautifully restored factory where Lt General Percival handed Singapore over to the Japanese in 1942 is an account of life in Singapore under Japanese occupation told through stories collected by the National Archives. The room where the surrender document was signed is the most powerful exhibit.
ⓐ 351 Upper Bukit Timah Rd ❶ 6332 7973 Ⓦ www.s1942.org.sg
🕘 09.00–17.30 Mon–Fri, 09.00–13.30 Sat Ⓝ Bus: 67, 75, 171, 173, 178, 184, 961, 170. Admission charge

Pulau Ubin

Pulau Ubin has more in common with a rural backwater in Malaysia than anywhere you would associate with Singapore, and a visit to the island is invariably a charming journey of discovery for most visitors. *Kampong* houses nestle in banana groves, with chickens running around and the occasional pig or goat rustling in the undergrowth. There are no cars and so far no plans to develop what must be a prime piece of real estate. The ideal way to get around is by bike, which can be hired from various shops such as **Comfort Bicycle Rental** (❶ 9008 1357), beside the boat jetty. There are places to eat near the jetty but take plenty of water on your cycle or trek around the island. Just as much fun is the bumboat ride out there. ❶ 6542 7944 Ⓝ Bus: 2 from Victoria St or Tanah Merah to Changi Village, then a boat from the nearby Changi Ferry Terminal (🕘 07.00–19.00) to the island

Singapore Zoo & Night Safari

As zoos go, this one is exemplary – happy-looking animals in

OUT OF TOWN

large enclosures, an endangered species breeding programme, and good contact between customer and exhibit. The animal shows are good fun and there are lots of things to engage younger visitors. The Night Safari adds the mystery of the dark to the enclosed animals. Wander around barely lit pathways to see nocturnal animals or take the tram ride through the various terrains set up in the park. ⓐ 80 Mandai Lake Rd, Bukit Timah ⓣ 6269 3411 ⓦ www.zoo.com.sg ⓛ Zoo: 08.30–18.00; Night

🔺 *Phor Kark See Temple*

BUKIT TIMAH, CHANGI & BINTAN

Safari: 19.30–00.00 ❷ MRT: Ang Mo Kio, then bus 138; Bus: 138, 171, 927. Admission charge for both sights

CULTURE

Phor Kark See Temple

Stretching over 8 hectares (19 acres) and standing out against the skyline with its multicoloured and decorated roofs, this Buddhist temple is quite modern but still fascinating to wander around. The monastery includes a library, refectory, crematorium, turtle ponds, pagodas and huge statues of the Buddha and Kuan Yin, the goddess of mercy. If the place seems a little familiar it is because several kung fu movies have been filmed using it as a backdrop. ⓐ 88 Bright Hill Dr, Bukit Timah ⓦ www.kmspks.org ⓛ 07.00–18.00 ❷ MRT: Bishan; Bus: 130

Sun Yat Sen Villa

A sight for lovers of Chinese history, this villa (near Toa Payoh) was home for a time to Dr Sun Yat Sen, who had a role to play in the Chinese revolution. You'll find pictures of Dr Sun rousing the tin miners of Malaysia, displays about his life and the history of the villa. ⓐ 12 Tai Gin Rd, Bukit Timah ⓣ 6256 7377 ⓦ www.wanqingyuan.com.sg ⓛ 09.00–17.00 Tues–Sun ❷ MRT: Toa Payoh; Bus: 21, 130, 131, 139, 145, 186. Admission charge

RETAIL THERAPY

Changi Airport So-called 'duty free' shopping at airports can be a scam but not, generally speaking, at Changi Airport. There are more than 100 shops in the departures and transit lounges of Terminals 1 and 2. Cutting Edge in Terminal 1 is good for gadgets and gizmos. ⏱ 07.00–22.00

Rumah Bebe A specialist beadwork and embroidery shop where you can be tempted by beaded slippers or a complete Peranakan wedding costume. Beading demonstrations are usually available but phone to check on times. ⓐ 113 East Coast Rd, Changi ⓘ 6247 8781 ⏱ 09.30–18.30 Tues–Sun Ⓜ MRT: Aljunied

TAKING A BREAK

Amigo £ At a weekend lunchtime it is not unusual to see a queue waiting for a dish of *laksa*, wanton noodles or *chicken chop hor fun* from Amigo. ⓐ 01-05 Changi Village Food Centre ⏱ 09.00–20.00 Ⓜ Bus: 2 from Victoria St or Tanah Merah to Changi Village

Mei Xiang Goreng Pisang Popiah £ This is the outlet to head for if you want delicious banana fritters cooked on the spot. The outlet at 01-31 offers an alternative snack in the form of carrot cake but it does not look or taste like what you might expect. ⓐ 01-15 Changi Village Food Centre ⏱ 09.00–20.00 Ⓜ Bus: 2 from Victoria St or Tanah Merah to Changi Village

First Stop Restaurant £–££ There are a couple of other places to eat on Pulau Ubin, but this is the most popular restaurant, partly because it has the widest choice of seafood and favourites like black pepper steak and sweet and sour chicken. A cold beer after a hot cycle goes down well here too. ⓐ Pulau Ubin, on the road by the jetty ⓣ 6543 2489 ⓛ 11.00–20.00 Thur–Tues ⓝ Bus: 2 from Victoria St or Tanah Merah to Changi Village, then a boat from the nearby Changi Ferry Terminal (ⓛ 07.00–19.00) to the island

Salt Water Café ££ This is the most comfortable setting for an evening meal in Changi and there is usually a seafood buffet, with international-style food as well, most evenings of the week. ⓐ Changi Village Hotel, 1 Netheravon Rd ⓣ 6379 7111 ⓛ 06.30–23.00 ⓝ Bus: 2 from Victoria St or Tanah Merah to Changi Village

AFTER DARK

Long Beach Seafood Restaurant ££ A famous seafood restaurant on the east coast where fresh fish are scooped out of the tanks and air-flown crabs from Alaska arrive at the kitchen packed in ice. The menu is extensive but some of the most popular choices are the chilli crabs and the lobster. The bamboo clam dish is rather special as well. ⓐ 1018 East Coast Parkway, Changi ⓣ 6445 8833 ⓦ www.longbeachseafood.com.sg ⓛ 11.00–15.00, 17.00–00.15 Sun–Fri, 11.00–15.00, 17.00–01.15 Sat ⓝ Bus: 401

ACCOMMODATION

Hotel 81 Joo Chiat £–££ See page 38 for details of this excellent chain of budget-priced hotels. This one, on Joo Chiat Road, is not the most conveniently located for the city centre but the

OUT OF TOWN

price difference would still allow for taxi rides, never mind public transport. ⓐ 305 Joo Chiat Rd, Changi ⓣ 6348 8181 ⓦ www.hotel81.com.sg Ⓝ MRT: Eunos

Changi Village Hotel ££–£££ Describing itself as 'minimalist chic', this smart-looking hotel with 380 rooms does have an uncluttered feel; it also faces the sea and has a spa. Relax in the swimming pool and gaze upwards at the planes using nearby Changi Airport. ⓐ Changi Village Hotel, 1 Netheravon Rd ⓣ 6379 7111 ⓦ www.changivillage.com.sg Ⓝ Bus: 2 from Victoria St or Tanah Merah to Changi Village

Nirwana Resort Hotel £££ A range of room types are available, along with a coffee shop, poolside restaurant, bistro and pub. You'll also find scuba diving, a gym and a jogging track. The contact information below also covers sister resorts including the similarly priced Mayang Sari and the five-star Indra Maya. ⓐ Bintan Island ⓣ Reservations: 6323 6636 ⓦ www.nirwanagardens.com Ⓝ Ferries from Tanah Merah Ferry Terminal (ⓣ 6542 4369 ⓦ www.brf.com.sg ⓛ 09.10–20.00 Mon–Thur, 08.10–20.00 Fri–Sun)

● *There are several tourist information centres to choose from*

PRACTICAL information

PRACTICAL INFORMATION

Directory

GETTING THERE
By air
Changi Airport (❶ 6542 1122 Ⓦ www.changi.airport.com.sg) is your most likely arrival point in the city. It has links to all major airports and is served by most major airlines as well as some local budget companies. Flying time from London is 13 hours, New York 18, Los Angeles 18 and Sydney 8.

Popular airlines flying to Singapore include:
Air France ❶ 6737 6355 Ⓦ www.airfrance.com
American Airlines ❶ 800 616 2113 Ⓦ www.aa.com
British Airways ❶ 6589 7000 Ⓦ www.ba.com
Malaysian Airlines ❶ 6336 6777 Ⓦ www.malaysiaairlines.com.my
Qantas ❶ 6589 7000 Ⓦ www.qantas.com.au
Silk Air ❶ 6225 4488 Ⓦ www.silkair.com
Singapore Airlines ❶ 6223 8888 Ⓦ www.singaporeair.com
United Airlines ❶ 6873 3533 Ⓦ www.united.com

Many people are aware that air travel emits CO_2, which contributes to climate change. You may be interested in lessening the environmental impact of your flight through the charity **Climate Care** (Ⓦ www.climatecare.org), which offsets your CO_2 by funding environmental projects around the world.

By rail
Singapore is connected via **KTM** (Ⓦ www.ktmb.com.my), the Malaysian rail service, to Malaysia and Thailand. The train station is at Keppel Road (❶ 6222 5156). Cab or bus 97 brings you into the city.

By road

Singapore is linked to Malaysia by two causeways. Buses arrive at the Johor Bahru causeway, and final destinations in Singapore include the Golden Mile Complex and Lavender Street. Coach services to destinations in Malaysia and Thailand depart from these bus stations. An alternative cheaper means of road travel to and from Singapore is to cross the Johor Bahru causeway on local buses 160, 170 or 950 and continue your journey from there.

By water

Several cruise ships arrive at the HarbourFront terminals. There are also ferries from the Indonesian islands which dock at the Tanah Merah Ferry Terminal (see page 117) or the HarbourFront terminals. From Tioman island off the east coast of Malaysia ferries arrive at the Tanah Merah Ferry Terminal.

ENTRY FORMALITIES

EU, US, Australian, New Zealand and Canadian citizens do not need a visa to enter Singapore. On arrival your passport will be stamped for a 14-day visit and you can ask for longer. Extensions for three months plus are possible through the Immigration Department. Another way to extend your stay in Singapore is to take a day trip into Johor Bahru. On return your passport will be stamped for another 14-day period.

You can bring into Singapore 1 litre of spirits, 1 litre of wine and 1 litre of beer. Duty is payable on all tobacco brought into the state. These restrictions do not apply if you enter the country from Malaysia (w www.customs.gov.sg).

PRACTICAL INFORMATION

The local currency is Singapore dollars

MONEY

The Singapore dollar is divided into 100 cents. Notes come in denominations of S$2, S$5, S$10, S$20, S$50, S$100, S$500, S$1,000 and S$10,000. Coins are in denominations of 1, 5, 10, 20 and 50 cents and S$1. There are S$1 notes in circulation, but these are rare and 1 cent coins are being decirculated but are still legal tender.

HEALTH, SAFETY & CRIME

There are very few health hazards to take into account when visiting Singapore. Water is safe to drink (it wouldn't dare not be!) and there are no inoculations required for entry.

If you are entering from an area where yellow fever is endemic, you may be asked to show proof of a recent vaccination against the disease. Hepatitis and typhoid inoculation might be worth considering, especially if you are travelling on to other destinations in Asia, and you should check that all your other vaccinations are up to date. Protection against malaria is not necessary in Singapore. Dengue fever is a minor risk in Singapore, and usually only found in the fast disappearing rural areas of the state.

Mosquito repellent is an essential requirement if you intend to visit any of the country park areas. Drinking water should be carried at all times and a sunhat is essential (Singaporeans often use umbrellas in the sun), as is sunscreen.

If you are bringing children, any medication should be brought with you. The hospital services, while not cheap, are excellent.

❶ Singapore does not have any reciprocal medical arrangements with other countries, so medical insurance is essential.

PRACTICAL INFORMATION

You will be as safe in Singapore as you are likely to be anywhere in the world. Pickpockets operate here but the usual precautions should keep you safe. Be aware of your valuables at all times and watch out for distractions – e.g. one person bumps into you while another helps themselves.

Your closest encounter with crime may occur when you commit one yourself. Jaywalking, smoking in certain places, spitting, eating on the MRT, chewing gum, urinating in lifts and littering are all offences that can incur an on-the-spot fine. Don't be confused by seeing Singaporeans jaywalking, littering or smoking and thinking that these laws are not imposed. The gay scene is an active and lively one although buggery, even between consenting adults in the privacy of their own home, is also illegal.

Overstaying your time on the island and possessing fireworks incur a caning, and having even tiny amounts of drugs incurs a long jail sentence. Drug trafficking is punished by the death penalty. Even having residual amounts of drugs in your system, consumed before entry to the state, is illegal.

OPENING HOURS

Shopping centres open 09.30–21.30; banks 09.30–15.00 Monday to Friday and 09.30–12.30 Saturday; and offices 08.30–17.00 Monday to Friday, 08.30–13.00 Saturday. Chinese temples operate more or less from dawn to dusk, while Hindu temples follow the same hours but close for an hour at noon. Mosques generally open 08.30–12.00 and 14.30–16.00.

DIRECTORY

TOILETS

Toilets, like drinking water, wouldn't dare be unclean. The best place to seek them out is in shopping malls, hotel lobbies, tourist sites, fast food outlets and hawker centres (although these can get a little messy because of the sheer volume of people using them). No one will mind or even notice you popping in. Most have at least one squat type toilet and you should carry tissues. There may be a charge of a few cents.

CHILDREN

Singapore is well aware of the spending power of children and there are any amount of activities to keep them busy. Just being around the wildlife in the parks and streets is fun, while the beaches and swimming pools are a blessed relief from shopping.

Eating out with children can also be an enjoyable experience. Hawker centres are great fun, fast food outlets are thick on the ground and there are so many inexpensive local dishes to try out. Restaurants welcome children, most have child seats and many have child menus.

Most tourist destinations have child reductions and hotels rarely charge a full rate for children under 12. There is no problem finding disposable nappies, baby food, bottles, etc.

The following are great places to take children:

Bukit Timah Nature Reserve (see page 117)
DUCKtours Take a ride around the city and its waterways in an amphibious vessel. ⓐ Suntec City ⓣ 6338 6877 ⓦ www.ducktours.com.sg ⓛ 10.00–18.00 ⓜ MRT: City Hall, then walk through Citylink Mall to Suntec City. Admission charge

PRACTICAL INFORMATION

East Coast Parkway Miles and miles of cycle paths, stretching along the southeastern coast of Singapore from Marina Promenade to the Tanah Merah Golf Course, with fast food places, rollerblades for hire, beaches, barbecues and more. Ⓝ Bus: 401

Escape Theme Park Big amusement park at Pasir Ris with 16 different scary rides. ⓐ 1 Pasir Ris Close ⓣ 6581 9112 ⓦ www.escapethemepark.com ⓛ 10.00–20.00 Sat, Sun & school holidays Ⓝ MRT: Pasir Ris

HIPPOtours Hop-on hop-off open top bus travelling around the various sights of Singapore. Takes the strain out of sightseeing. Five different tours including evenings. ⓐ Suntec City ⓣ 6338 6877 ⓦ www.ducktours.com.sg ⓛ City hop-on hop-off tour: 10.00–17.30; evening hop-on hop-off tour: 18.00–22.00; Sentosa hop-on hop-off tour: 10.00–21.00 Ⓝ MRT: City Hall, then walk through Citylink Mall to Suntec City. Admission charge

Jurong Bird Park (see page 108)

Kart World Go-karting fun for those aged eight and over. ⓐ Behind KFC in Yung Ho Rd, Taman Jurong ⓣ 6266 2555 ⓦ www.kartworld.com.sg ⓛ 11.00–19.00 Tues–Sun Ⓝ MRT: Lakeside, then bus 154. Admission charge

MINT Museum of Toys Five floors of vintage toys and, of course, a shop. ⓐ 26 Seah St ⓣ 6339 0660 ⓦ www.emint.com ⓛ 09.30–18.30 Ⓝ MRT: City Hall. Admission charge

Pulau Ubin (see page 119)

Sentosa (see page 109)

Singapore Science Centre (see page 111)

Singapore Zoo (see page 119)

Sungei Buloh Wetland Reserve Choose from a number of walks,

DIRECTORY

Children love DUCKtours' novel bus-cum-boat ride

PRACTICAL INFORMATION

from 500 m (550 yards) to 7 km (4 miles), around this amazing nature reserve, to see mangroves and mangrove wildlife.
ⓐ 301 Neo Tiew Crescent ⓣ 6794 1401 ⓦ www.sbwr.org.sg
ⓑ 07.30–19.00 Mon–Sat, 07.00–19.00 Sun & public holidays
ⓝ Bus: 925 from Kranji MRT station. Admission free on weekdays

Wild Wild Wet Right next door to the Escape Theme Park, this is a series of water rides, pools, etc. ⓐ 1 Pasir Ris Close ⓣ 6581 9128 ⓦ www.wildwildwet.com ⓑ 13.00–19.00 Mon, Wed–Fri, 10.00–17.00 Sat & Sun ⓝ MRT: Pasir Ris. Admission charge

ⓘ Remember to keep children covered with sun hats and sunscreen, and make sure they have lots of water to drink. Mosquito repellent is essential in country and city parks.

COMMUNICATIONS
Internet
Internet cafés are becoming rare in Singapore (as in other countries) since everyone is connected to broadband at home, work or school. Libraries have internet stations, and Starbucks, McDonald's, Coffeebean cafés and other locations have free wireless connection. Some public areas of the city also have wireless connection.

Phone
Public telephones are located around the island and take either coins, phone cards or credit cards. A three-minute local call costs 10 cents. Coin phones take only small denomination coins and can mostly only be used for local calls. Cards for card phones come in denominations of S$3, S$5, S$10, S$20 and S$50, and

DIRECTORY

> **TELEPHONING SINGAPORE**
> To telephone Singapore from abroad, dial the international access code first (00), then the country code for Singapore (65), followed by the eight-digit number.
>
> **TELEPHONING ABROAD**
> To make an international call from Singapore, dial 001, then the country code, followed by the local area code minus the first 0, and finally the number. Country codes:
> **Australia** 61
> **Canada & USA** 1
> **New Zealand** 64
> **Republic of Ireland** 353
> **South Africa** 27
> **UK** 44

can be bought at post offices and some shops. Used phone cards are highly collectible.

Mobile phones are widely used. If you have a GSM 900 or GSM 1800 phone, you can buy a prepaid SIM card to use while in Singapore. However, American mobile phone users will need to hire a phone or buy a second-hand one for use while in Singapore.

Three phone companies operate in Singapore; each has different rates for outgoing calls and mobile phone hire and rates:
M1 🌐 www.m1.com.sg
SingTel 🌐 www.singtel.com
Starhub 🌐 www.starhub.com

PRACTICAL INFORMATION

Post
The main post office is at Eunos Road 8, but there are sub post offices in most of the big shopping centres. The Eunos Road PO has a *poste restante*. Airmail letters start at S$1.10 and postcards cost 50 cents. ☎ 1606 (for the nearest branch to you) ⓦ www.singpost.com ⏰ 08.30–17.00 Mon–Fri, 08.30–13.00 Sat.

ELECTRICITY
Mains electricity is 220–240 V 50 Hz. Plugs are uniformly three square pins, although lots of electrical appliances come with a two-pin plug. Adaptors are readily available.

TRAVELLERS WITH DISABILITIES
Travellers with disabilities will do fairly well in Singapore. Most modern hotels have wheelchair access and specially designed rooms, although advance notice is necessary to get one. The MRT might prove a problem for wheelchair users, but most shopping centres have ramps and lifts. Road crossings have an aural signal as well as a visual one.

Visit ⓦ www.dpa.org.sg – a useful website to check before arriving. It lists cinemas, shopping centres and many other places with an account of their facilities for travellers with disabilities. **Smart Taxis** (☎ 6555 8888 ⓦ www.smrttaxis.com.sg) has London black cab-style taxis adapted for wheelchair users. All taxis must be booked in advance, allowing 24 hours at least.

TOURIST INFORMATION
Tourist offices
Changi Airport ⓐ Arrivals lounge in Terminals 1, 2 & 3

DIRECTORY

🕐 06.00–02.00 Ⓜ MRT: Changi
Cruise Centre @ Arrivals lounge, Cruise Centre, HarbourFront
🕐 24 hours Ⓜ MRT: HarbourFront
Liang Court @ 177 River Valley Rd, Level 1 Liang Court Shopping Centre 🕐 10.30–21.30 Ⓜ MRT: Clarke Quay
Little India @ 73 Dunlop St 🕐 10.00–22.00 Ⓜ MRT: Little India
Orchard @ Junction of Orchard Rd & Cairnhill Rd
🕐 09.30–22.30 Ⓜ MRT: Orchard
Suntec @ The Galleria, Suntec City Mall 🕐 10.00–18.00
Ⓜ MRT: City Hall
24-hour tourist hotline ☎ 1800 736 2000 within Singapore and 65 6736 2000 outside Singapore
🌐 www.visitsingapore.com

BACKGROUND READING

Asian Flavours by Connie Clarkson. Singaporean hawker-style recipes.
King Rat by James Clavell. Account of the misery of survival in Changi prisoner of war camp.
Rogue Trader by Nick Leeson. Account by the infamous rogue trader of his exploits in Singapore.
Singapore Grip by JG Farrell. Novel set in pre-Japanese occupied Singapore.
Street Smart Singapore by David Brazil. Lots of fascinating stories about the city state.
The Syonan Years by Lee Geok Boi. A very readable and generously illustrated book about Singapore during World War II.

PRACTICAL INFORMATION

Emergencies

EMERGENCY NUMBERS
The following are emergency free-call numbers:
Ambulance and fire brigade 995
Police 999

MEDICAL SERVICES
Alexandra Hospital Alexandra Rd 6472 2000
Gleneagles 6A Napier Rd 6470 5700
Mount Alvernia 820 Thomson Rd 6347 6210
Mount Elizabeth 3 Mount Elizabeth 6731 2218
Raffles Hospital 585 North Bridge Rd 6311 1555
Singapore General Hospital Outram Rd 6321 4311

OTHER USEFUL NUMBERS
Flight information 1800 542 4422 (toll free)
Drug & Poison Information Centre 6423 9119 (toll free)
Singapore Tourist Board complaints hotline 1800 736 3366 (toll free)
Touristline 1800 736 2000 (toll free)

Lost or stolen credit cards
American Express 6880 1111
MasterCard 800 110 0113
Visa 800 448 1250

EMBASSIES & CONSULATES
Australia 25 Napier Rd 6836 4100

EMERGENCIES

Canada ⓐ 15th Floor IBM Tower, 80 Anson Rd ⓣ 6325 3240
UK ⓐ 100 Tanglin Rd ⓣ 6424 4200
USA ⓐ 27 Napier Rd ⓣ 6476 9100

🔺 *Colonial charm at the Central Fire Station on Hill Street*

INDEX

A

accommodation 37–41
 Changi & Bintan 123–4
 Sentosa & Western Singapore 115
air travel 50–1, 126
airport 50–1, 121–2, 126
Amoy Street 91
Arab Street 37, 76
arts *see* culture
Asian Civilisations Museum 65

B

bamboo & paper goods 95
bars & clubs 30–1, 71, 74–5, 89, 102
 see also nightlife
Battle Box 44, 49, 66
beer 111
Bintan 116–17
Boat Quay 31, 42, 90
boat travel 127, 131
Botanic Gardens 44, 46, 104–5
Buddhism 11, 81, 121
Bukit Timah Nature Reserve 42, 116, 117–18
bus travel 51, 55, 58, 127, 132

C

cable-car 105, 108
cafés
 Boat Quay & Chinatown 100
 Changi & Bintan 122–3
 Little India & Arab Street 86
 Orchard Road & Colonial District 70–1
 Sentosa & Western Singapore 112–13
car hire 58
Changi 46–7, 118
Changi Museum 118
Chijmes 89
children 69, 104, 111, 129, 131–4
Chinatown 24, 42, 44, 54, 90–9
Chinatown Heritage Centre 95–6
Chinese New Year 11
Chinese opera 12, 13, 20
cinema 32, 33, 49, 75, 136
Clarke Quay 30, 32, 44
climate 10, 48–9, 54
Colonial District 60–5
crafts 24, 67, 99, 108, 112
cricket 34
crime 17, 54, 129–30
culture 11–13, 20–2, 65–7, 75, 80–3, 95–9, 110–11, 121
customs & duty 121, 127
cycling 34–5, 119, 132

D

dance 20
death houses 91, 96
Deepavali 12, 83

department stores 24–5, 68, 80
disabilities 136
Dragon Boat Festival 11
driving 51, 58

E

East Coast Parkway 132
electricity 136
embassies & consulates 138–9
emergencies 138–9
entertainment 30–3, 49, 75, 109, 110, 131–2
 see also nightlife
Esplanade – Theatres on the Bay 20, 43, 45, 46, 60, 75
Eu Yan Sang Medical Hall 95, 96
events 11–15, 83
ez-link card 55

F

Far East Square 91
fashion 24, 68
festivals 11–15, 83
Festival of the Hungry Ghosts 12
food & drink 18–19, 26–9, 31, 71–4, 86–9, 100–2, 112–15
football 34
Fort Canning Hill 60–1
Fort Siloso 110

INDEX

Fu Tak Chi Museum 98

G
go-karting 132
golf 35–6

H
HarbourFront 105, 108, 126
Haw Par Villa 104, 110
hawker centres 26, 28, 33, 45, 49, 96, 105, 131
health 129, 138
Hinduism 12–13, 14–15, 81–3, 95, 97, 130
history 16–17, 66–7, 118–19, 121
Holland Village 104, 108
hostels 37, 41
hotels
 see accommodation

I
Images of Singapore Exhibition 110–11
insurance 129
internet 134
Islam 13, 83
Istana Kampong Glam 80–1

J
Joo Chiat Road 118
Jurong Bird Park 108

K
Kranji War Cemetery 118

L
legislation 17, 54, 130
lifestyle 18–19
lion dancers 20
Little India 37, 54, 76, 80–3
Little India Conservation Area 77
Long Bar 70

M
MacRitchie Reservoir Park 46
malls 49, 68–70
markets 12, 44, 49, 94, 108
Memories at Old Ford Factory 119
MINT Museum of Toys 132
Moon Cake Festival 12
money 128
monorail 105
Mount Faber 105, 108
MRT (Mass Rapid Transit) 50, 55
music 12, 13, 20, 22, 31–2, 80

N
National Day 12
National Museum of Singapore 67
Navarathiri 13
Night Safari 119–20
nightlife 30–3
 Boat Quay & Chinatown 102
 Little India & Arab Street 89

 Orchard Road & Colonial District 74–5
 Sentosa & Western Singapore 115
NUS Museum 46

O
opening hours 33, 130
Orchard Road 24, 43, 44, 48, 54, 60–1, 68–9
orchids 105

P
Padang 64
Pagoda Street 99
parks & gardens 46–7, 60–1, 104–5, 108
passports & visas 127
phones 134–5
Phor Kark See Temple 121
post 136
public holidays 13
public transport 50–1, 55–8, 127
Pulau Ubin 42, 119

Q
Qing Ming Festival 11

R
Raffles, Sir Thomas Stamford 16, 64
Raffles Hotel 43, 64, 70
Raffles Hotel Museum 67
Raffles' Landing Site 64
rail travel 51, 126
rainforest 117–18

INDEX

Ramadan 12
reading 137
restaurants 26–9
  Boat Quay &
    Chinatown 100–1
  Changi 122
  Little India &
    Arab Street 87–9
  Orchard Road &
    Colonial District 72–4
  Sentosa & Western
    Singapore 113–15
road travel 8, 51, 54–5, 58, 127, 136

S

safety 54, 129
Sago Street 91, 94, 100
Sakaya Muni Buddha
  Gaya Temple 81
sea travel 127
seafood 18, 122–3
Sentosa 11, 43, 47, 55, 104, 109
Serangoon Road 77, 80
shopping 19, 24–5, 46, 49
  Boat Quay &
    Chinatown 94–5, 99–100
  Changi 121–2
  Little India &
    Arab Street 76, 80, 84–5
  Orchard Road &
    Colonial District 67–70
  Sentosa & Western
    Singapore 108, 112
Sin Chor Kung Temple 91
Singapore City Gallery 98
Singapore Flyer 65
Singapore Grand Prix 12
Singapore River 54
Singapore Science
  Centre 111
Singapore Sling 70
Singapore Zoo 119–20, 132
South Bridge Road 95
spas 36
sport & activities 34–6, 65, 132–4
Sri Mariamman Temple 97
Sri Srinivasa Perumal
  Temple 14, 81
Sri Veeramakaliamman
  Temple 81–2
Sultan Mosque 83
Sun Yat Sen Villa 121
symbols &
  abbreviations 6

T

tailoring 24
Taoism 98
tax 25
taxis 51, 58, 136
Thaipusam 14–15
Thian Hock Keng
  Temple 43, 99
Thimithi 13
Tiger Brewery 111
time differences 50
toilets 131
tourist information 136–7
tours 41, 47, 60, 80, 96, 111, 131–2
travel passes 55, 58
Trengganu Street 94
Trishaw Park 94

V

Vesak Day 11
VivoCity 112

W

Western Singapore 104–11
wetmarkets 49, 94, 108

Z

zoo 119–20, 132

SPOTTED YOUR NEXT CITY BREAK?

... then these CitySpots will have you in the know in no time, wherever you're heading.

Covering 100 cities worldwide, these vibrant pocket guides are packed with practical listings and imaginative suggestions, making sure you get the most out of your break, whatever your taste or budget.

Aarhus	Geneva	Paris
Amsterdam	Genoa	Pisa
Antwerp	Glasgow	Prague
Athens	Gothenburg	Porto
Bangkok	Granada	Reims
Barcelona	Hamburg	Reykjavik
Belfast	Hanover	Riga
Belgrade	Helsinki	Rome
Berlin	Hong Kong	Rotterdam
Biarritz	Istanbul	Salzburg
Bilbao	Kiev	San Francisco
Bologna	Krakow	Sarajevo
Bordeaux	Kuala Lumpur	Seville
Bratislava	Leipzig	Singapore
Bruges	Lille	Sofia
Brussels	Lisbon	Split
Bucharest	Liverpool	Stockholm
Budapest	Ljubljana	Strasbourg
Cairo	London	St Petersburg
Cape Town	Los Angeles	Tallinn
Cardiff	Lyon	Tirana
Cologne	Madrid	Tokyo
Copenhagen	Marrakech	Toulouse
Cork	Marseilles	Turin
Delhi	Milan	Valencia
Dubai	Monte Carlo	Venice
Dublin	Moscow	Verona
Dubrovnik	Munich	Vienna
Düsseldorf	Naples	Vilnius
Edinburgh	New York City	Warsaw
Fez	Nice	Zagreb
Florence	Oslo	Zurich
Frankfurt	Palermo	
Gdansk	Palma	

Available from all good bookshops, your local Thomas Cook travel store or browse and buy online at www.thomascookpublishing.com

Thomas Cook Publishing

ACKNOWLEDGEMENTS & FEEDBACK

Editorial/project management: Lisa Plumridge
Copy editor: Paul Hines
Layout/DTP: Alison Rayner

The publishers would like to thank the following individuals and organisations for supplying their copyright photographs for this book: Chung Yin Kwong/BigStockPhoto.com, pages 30–1; Edwin Lee, page 139; Gene Lee, page 88; Pat Levy, pages 9, 19, 25, 27, 39, 40, 50, 59, 61, 73, 77 & 125; Modery, page 117; Pictures Colour Library, pages 1, 21, 23, 42–3, 45, 48 & 103; Singapore DUCKtours Pte Ltd, page 133; Singapore Tourism Board, pages 7, 10, 15, 29, 35, 47 & 109; Alvin Teo/Dreamstime.com, page 128; Bernard Tey, page 90; Wikimedia (Terence Ong, pages 66, 82 & 120; Sengkang, page 94; CalvinTeo, page 104).

Send your thoughts to
books@thomascook.com

- **Found a great bar, club, shop or must-see sight that we don't feature?**
- **Like to tip us off about any information that needs a little updating?**
- **Want to tell us what you love about this handy little guidebook and more importantly how we can make it even handier?**

Then here's your chance to tell all! Send us ideas, discoveries and recommendations today and then look out for your valuable input in the next edition of this title.

Email the above address (stating the title) or write to:
CitySpots Series Editor, Thomas Cook Publishing, PO Box 227, Coningsby Road, Peterborough PE3 8SB, UK.